fast
slow

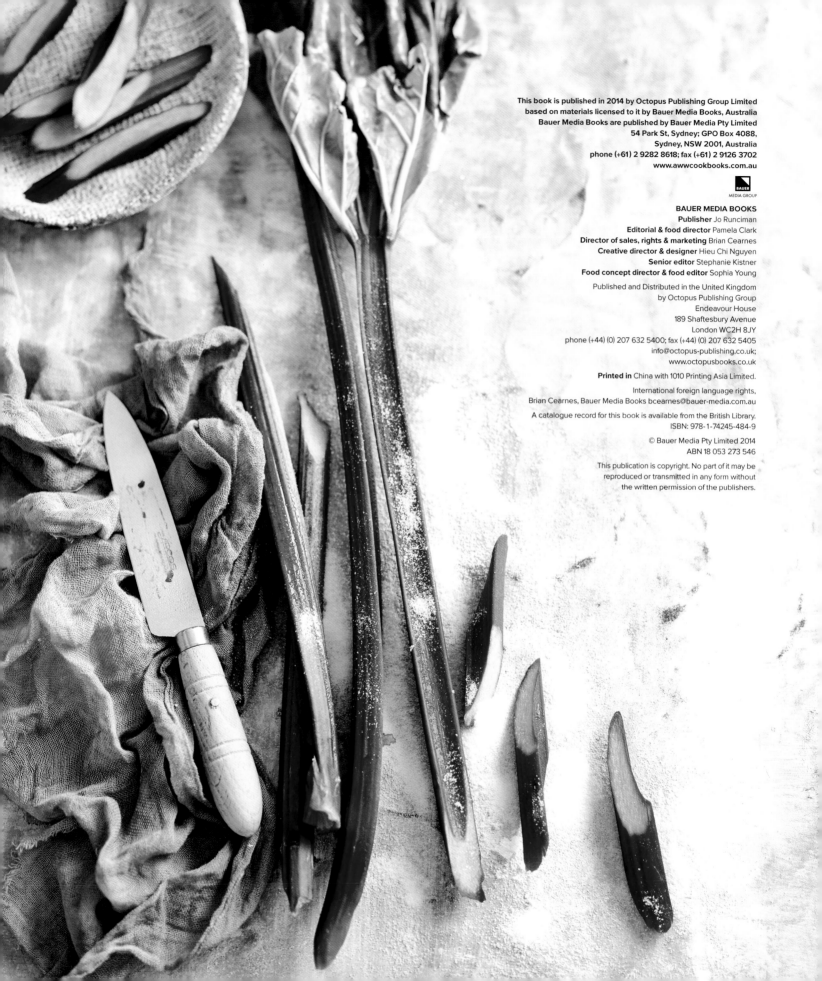

This book is published in 2014 by Octopus Publishing Group Limited
based on materials licensed to it by Bauer Media Books, Australia
Bauer Media Books are published by Bauer Media Pty Limited
54 Park St, Sydney; GPO Box 4088,
Sydney, NSW 2001, Australia
phone (+61) 2 9282 8618; fax (+61) 2 9126 3702
www.awwcookbooks.com.au

BAUER MEDIA BOOKS
Publisher Jo Runciman
Editorial & food director Pamela Clark
Director of sales, rights & marketing Brian Cearnes
Creative director & designer Hieu Chi Nguyen
Senior editor Stephanie Kistner
Food concept director & food editor Sophia Young

Published and Distributed in the United Kingdom
by Octopus Publishing Group
Endeavour House
189 Shaftesbury Avenue
London WC2H 8JY
phone (+44) (0) 207 632 5400; fax (+44) (0) 207 632 5405
info@octopus-publishing.co.uk;
www.octopusbooks.co.uk

Printed in China with 1010 Printing Asia Limited.

International foreign language rights,
Brian Cearnes, Bauer Media Books bcearnes@bauer-media.com.au

A catalogue record for this book is available from the British Library.
ISBN: 978-1-74245-484-9

© Bauer Media Pty Limited 2014
ABN 18 053 273 546

THE AUSTRALIAN Women's Weekly

fast
slow

CONTENTS

FAST LUNCHES

YOU CAN TAKE THIS SALAD TO WORK FOR LUNCH. PACKAGE THE BREAD AND SALAD IN SEPARATE CONTAINERS; KEEP SALAD IN THE FRIDGE AND BREAD AT ROOM TEMPERATURE. TOSS TOGETHER JUST BEFORE YOU'RE READY TO EAT.

ROAST BEEF & PANZANELLA SALAD

PREP + COOK TIME 20 MINUTES

SERVES 2

150G (4½ OUNCES) CIABATTA BREAD

⅓ CUP (80ML) OLIVE OIL

1 CLOVE GARLIC, CRUSHED

2 TABLESPOONS RED WINE VINEGAR

170G (5½ OUNCES) GRAPE TOMATOES, HALVED

150G (4½ OUNCES) BOTTLED ROASTED RED CAPSICUM (BELL PEPPER), DRAINED, CHOPPED COARSELY

½ CUP LIGHTLY PACKED FRESH BASIL LEAVES, TORN IN HALF

⅓ CUP (50G) PITTED BLACK OLIVES

1 TABLESPOON DRAINED BABY CAPERS, RINSED

100G (3 OUNCES) RARE ROAST BEEF SLICES

1 Preheat oven to 200°C/400°F. Line an oven tray with baking paper.

2 Tear bread into bite-sized pieces. Place bread in a single layer on tray; drizzle with half the oil. Bake 10 minutes or until golden.

3 Place garlic, vinegar and remaining oil in a screw-top jar; shake well. Season to taste.

4 Place tomatoes, capsicum, basil, olives and capers in a large bowl with bread; toss gently to combine. Top with beef; drizzle with dressing.

nutritional count per serving *43.4g total fat (6.5g saturated fat); 2719kJ (650 cal); 40.6g carbohydrate; 19.6g protein; 6.5g fibre*

ROAST PUMPKIN & CHICKPEA SALAD

1 Preheat oven to 200°C/400°F.

2 Combine pumpkin and oil in a large roasting pan; season. Roast for 15 minutes or until tender.

3 Meanwhile, place nuts on an oven tray; roast, in oven, for 3 minutes or until golden. Remove from tray immediately.

4 Make preserved lemon vinaigrette.

5 Place pumpkin in a large bowl with chickpeas, onion, spinach leaves and vinaigrette; toss gently to combine. Serve salad sprinkled with nuts, fetta and chives.

PRESERVED LEMON VINAIGRETTE Place ingredients in a screw-top jar; shake well.

PREP + COOK TIME 30 MINUTES

SERVES 4

1.3KG (2¾ POUNDS) BUTTERNUT PUMPKIN, PEELED, CHOPPED COARSELY

1 TABLESPOON OLIVE OIL

¼ CUP (35G) PISTACHIOS

400G (12½ OUNCES) CANNED CHICKPEAS (GARBANZO BEANS), DRAINED, RINSED

1 SMALL RED ONION (100G), SLICED THINLY

150G (4½ OUNCES) BABY SPINACH LEAVES

100G (3 OUNCES) FETTA, CRUMBLED

1 TABLESPOON COARSELY CHOPPED FRESH CHIVES

PRESERVED LEMON VINAIGRETTE

1 CLOVE GARLIC, CRUSHED

2 TEASPOONS FINELY CHOPPED PRESERVED LEMON RIND

2 TABLESPOONS OLIVE OIL

1½ TABLESPOONS WHITE WINE VINEGAR

YOU WILL NEED 1 WEDGE PRESERVED LEMON FOR THE AMOUNT OF FINELY CHOPPED RIND REQUIRED. REMOVE AND DISCARD THE FLESH FROM THE WEDGE, THEN RINSE THE RIND WELL BEFORE CHOPPING.

nutritional count per serving *35g total fat (8.1g saturated fat); 2231kJ (533 cal); 34.1g carbohydrate; 15.5g protein; 12.4g fibre*

SWEET CHILLI CHICKEN WITH MANGO LIME SALAD

PREP + COOK TIME 20 MINUTES

SERVES 4

4 CHICKEN BREAST FILLETS (800G)

2 TABLESPOONS OLIVE OIL

½ CUP (125ML) SWEET CHILLI SAUCE

1 CLOVE GARLIC, CRUSHED

2 TABLESPOONS LIME JUICE

100G (3 OUNCES) ROCKET (ARUGULA)

2 LIMES (180G), HALVED

MANGO LIME SALAD

2 MEDIUM MANGOES (860G), SLICED THINLY

1 SMALL RED ONION (100G), SLICED THINLY

2 TABLESPOONS LIME JUICE

1 LONG FRESH RED CHILLI, CHOPPED FINELY

1 Heat an oiled chargrill pan (or barbecue or grill) over medium heat.

2 Cut chicken breasts in half lengthways. Combine chicken with oil, sweet chilli sauce, garlic and juice in a medium bowl; season.

3 Cook chicken in chargrill pan, in two batches, for 2 minutes each side or until cooked through.

4 Meanwhile, make mango lime salad.

5 Serve chicken with rocket, mango lime salad and lime halves. Drizzle with cooking juices.

MANGO LIME SALAD Place ingredients in a medium bowl; toss gently to combine.

WE USED ROCKET SOLD IN BUNCHES – IT HAS A MORE PEPPERY TASTE THAN LOOSE BABY ROCKET. IF FRESH MANGO IS NOT AVAILABLE, YOU CAN USE 800G (1½ POUNDS) CANNED MANGO CHEEKS INSTEAD; DRAIN THEM WELL, THEN SLICE THINLY.

nutritional count per serving *13.6g total fat (2.5g saturated fat); 1760kJ (421 cal); 24.1g carbohydrate; 47.4g protein; 4.2g fibre*

WE'VE DELIBERATELY MADE THIS FAST AND SATISIFYING RECIPE WITHOUT OIL IN ORDER TO MAKE IT LOW FAT, SO IDEALLY YOU NEED TO USE A NON-STICK SAUCEPAN. YOU COULD, HOWEVER, USE A REGULAR PAN AND SPRAY IT WITH A LITTLE COOKING OIL.

CHICKEN & CORN SOUP

1 Cut kernels from corn cob.

2 Heat a large non-stick saucepan over medium heat; cook corn kernels with ginger, garlic and half the green onion, stirring, until fragrant.

3 Add creamed corn, soy sauce and stock; bring to the boil. Add chicken. Reduce heat; simmer, uncovered, 10 minutes. Gradually stir in egg white. Season to taste.

4 Serve soup topped with remaining green onion.

TIPS If you don't have salt-reduced chicken stock, replace 1 cup of the stock with water. You will need to buy a barbecued chicken weighing about 900g (1¾ pounds) for this recipe. Any leftover chicken can be used in sandwiches.

PREP + COOK TIME 25 MINUTES

SERVES 2

1 TRIMMED CORN COB (250G)

1½ TEASPOONS FINELY GRATED GINGER

1 CLOVE GARLIC, CRUSHED

2 GREEN ONIONS (SCALLIONS), SLICED THINLY

250G (8 OUNCES) CANNED CREAMED CORN

1 TABLESPOON JAPANESE SOY SAUCE

1 LITRE (4 CUPS) SALT-REDUCED CHICKEN STOCK

2 CUPS (320G) CHOPPED SKINLESS COOKED CHICKEN

1 EGG WHITE, BEATEN LIGHTLY

nutritional count per serving *5.6g total fat (1.6g saturated fat); 1513kJ (362 cal); 44g carbohydrate; 50.2g protein; 9g fibre*

WHEN SEASONING SOUTH EAST ASIAN RECIPES, SUCH AS THIS PORK LARB, ADJUST THE SWEET (BROWN SUGAR), SOUR (LIME JUICE) AND SALTY (FISH SAUCE) INGREDIENTS TO CREATE A BALANCED TASTE.

PORK LARB WITH RICE NOODLES

PREP + COOK TIME 20 MINUTES

SERVES 4

200G (6½ OUNCES) RICE STICK NOODLES

1 TABLESPOON PEANUT OIL

600G (1¼ POUNDS) MINCED (GROUND) PORK

10CM (4-INCH) STALK FRESH LEMON GRASS (20G), CHOPPED FINELY

1 CLOVE GARLIC, CRUSHED

2 TEASPOONS SAMBAL OELEK

2 TABLESPOONS LIME JUICE

2 TABLESPOONS BROWN SUGAR

1 TABLESPOON FISH SAUCE

3 GREEN ONIONS (SCALLIONS), SLICED THINLY

1 FRESH LONG RED CHILLI, SLICED THINLY

¼ CUP LOOSELY PACKED FRESH CORIANDER (CILANTRO) LEAVES

1 LIME (90G), CUT INTO CHEEKS

1 Cook noodles in a medium saucepan of boiling water until tender; drain.

2 Meanwhile, heat oil in a large frying pan over high heat; cook pork, stirring, until browned. Add lemon grass, garlic and sambal oelek; cook stirring, 1 minute or until fragrant. Add juice, sugar and fish sauce; cook for 1 minute. Remove from heat; stir in green onion.

3 Serve pork mixture on noodles topped with chilli and coriander; accompany with lime cheeks.

TIPS Rice stick noodles, are sometimes sold as pad thai noodles and are available from the Asian food section in supermarkets. Sambal oelek is a hot chilli paste, available from major supermarkets and Asian food stores. You can use 1 small seeded, finely chopped red chilli or ½ teaspoon chilli flakes instead.

nutritional count per serving *18.9g total fat (6g saturated fat); 1546kJ (369 cal); 16.6g carbohydrate; 32.9g protein; 0.9g fibre*

SALT & FIVE-SPICE CRISP CHICKEN

1 Heat oil in a large frying pan or wok over medium-high heat.

2 Cut chicken into 2cm (¾-inch) slices. Combine flour, spices and salt in a large bowl; add chicken, toss to coat.

3 Shallow-fry chicken, in three batches, for 2 minutes each side or until browned lightly and cooked through. Drain on paper towel.

4 Meanwhile, combine mirin and oil in a small bowl, then add chilli, green onion, bean sprouts and ginger; toss gently to combine.

5 Serve chicken with bean sprout mixture, aïoli and lime wedges.

TIP For shallow-frying, add enough oil to come halfway up the side of the food to be fried.

PREP + COOK TIME 20 MINUTES

SERVES 4

VEGETABLE OIL, FOR SHALLOW-FRYING

800G (1½ POUNDS) CHICKEN THIGH FILLETS

⅓ CUP (45G) RICE FLOUR

1 TABLESPOON CHINESE FIVE SPICE

¼ TEASPOON CAYENNE PEPPER

1 TEASPOON SALT

¼ CUP (60ML) MIRIN

1 TEASPOON SESAME OIL

1 LONG FRESH GREEN CHILLI, SLICED THINLY

2 GREEN ONIONS (SCALLIONS), SLICED THINLY

1 CUP (80G) BEAN SPROUTS, TRIMMED

1 TABLESPOON THINLY SHREDDED GINGER

⅓ CUP (75G) AÏOLI

1 LIME (90G), CUT INTO WEDGES

AÏOLI IS GARLIC MAYONNAISE, AVAILABLE FROM THE CONDIMENT AISLE IN MOST SUPERMARKETS. YOU CAN MAKE YOUR OWN QUICK VERSION BY STIRRING 1 CRUSHED CLOVE GARLIC INTO ⅓ CUP (75G) WHOLE-EGG MAYONNAISE.

nutritional count per serving 40.6g total fat (8.1g saturated fat); 2520kJ (602 cal); 17.3g carbohydrate; 39.1g protein; 0.8g fibre

BEEF & MIXED SPROUT SALAD

PREP + COOK TIME 30 MINUTES

SERVES 4

2 TEASPOONS FINELY GRATED FRESH GINGER

2 CLOVES GARLIC, CRUSHED

1 TABLESPOON SOY SAUCE

2 TABLESPOONS OLIVE OIL

600G (1¼ POUNDS) BEEF RUMP STEAK

250G (8 OUNCES) BABY SPINACH LEAVES

1 MEDIUM CARROT (120G), GRATED COARSELY

½ CUP (20G) ALFALFA SPROUTS

½ CUP (25G) SNOW PEA SPROUTS

SOY LIME DRESSING

2 TABLESPOONS LIME JUICE

1 TABLESPOON OLIVE OIL

1 TABLESPOON SOY SAUCE

1 Combine ginger, garlic, soy sauce and half the oil in a medium bowl; add beef, turn to coat in marinade.

2 Cook beef on a heated oiled chargrill plate (or barbecue or grill) for 3 minutes each side or until cooked as desired. Remove from heat, cover; rest 10 minutes.

3 Meanwhile, make soy lime dressing.

4 Cut beef into thin slices. Arrange beef slices on a platter with spinach leaves, carrot and sprouts; drizzle with dressing.

SOY LIME DRESSING Place ingredients in a screw-top jar; shake well.

TIP For rare beef, cook for a few mintues each side. For medium-rare, cook on one side until moisture is just visible on top, turn and repeat on the other side. For medium, cook on one side until moisture is pooling on top. Cook on the second side until surface moisture is visible. For medium-well done meat, increase the cooking time on both sides, to test for doneness press with the side of tongs; the meat will feel firm with a slight springiness. Well done steak will feel quite firm when pressed.

nutritional count per serving *28g total fat (7.5g saturated fat); 2012kJ (481 cal); 2.8g carbohydrate; 53g protein; 2.8g fibre*

THAI BEEF SALAD

1 Heat vegetable oil in a medium frying pan over medium-high heat; cook beef for 4 minutes each side or until cooked as desired. Remove from heat, cover; rest 5 minutes.

2 Meanwhile, whisk rind, juice, chilli, fish sauce, sugar and sesame oil in a small bowl until combined.

3 Slice beef thinly. Place beef in a large bowl with half the dressing; toss gently to combine.

4 Segment grapefruit (see tip). Add segments to beef mixture with cucumber, tomato, onion, herbs and remaining dressing; toss gently to combine. Season to taste. Serve salad topped with coconut.

TIPS You will need 1 lime for this recipe. To segment grapefruit, cut off the rind with the white pith, following the curve of the fruit. Cut down either side of each segment close to the membrane to release the segment.

PREP + COOK TIME 15 MINUTES

SERVES 4

1 TABLESPOON VEGETABLE OIL

500G (1 POUND) BEEF SIRLOIN STEAK, TRIMMED

1 TEASPOON FINELY GRATED LIME RIND

2 TABLESPOONS LIME JUICE

1 FRESH SMALL RED CHILLI, SLICED THINLY LENGTHWAYS

2 TABLESPOONS FISH SAUCE

1 TABLESPOON GRATED PALM SUGAR

2 TABLESPOONS SESAME OIL

1 MEDIUM GRAPEFRUIT (425G)

1 TELEGRAPH CUCUMBER (400G), SLICED THINLY

2 MEDIUM TOMATOES (300G), SLICED THINLY

1 MEDIUM RED ONION (170G), SLICED THINLY

1 CUP LOOSELY PACKED FRESH MINT LEAVES

1 CUP LOOSELY PACKED FRESH BASIL LEAVES

¼ CUP (10G) FLAKED COCONUT

THE BEST WAY TO STORE FRESH HERBS IS AS YOU WOULD A BUNCH OF FLOWERS. TRIM THE STEMS SLIGHTLY, THEN PLACE IN A JUG OR GLASS OF WATER. STORE OUT OF THE FRIDGE, COVERED WITH A PLASTIC BAG. CHANGE THE WATER DAILY AND THEY CAN LAST FOR UP TO 2 WEEKS.

nutritional count per serving *19.9g total fat (4.7g saturated fat); 1606kJ (384 cal); 13.5g carbohydrate; 34.7g protein; 5.3g fibre*

BLUE CHEESE, APPLE & BARBECUED CHICKEN SLAW

PREP + COOK TIME 30 MINUTES

SERVES 4

⅓ CUP (45G) FLAKED ALMONDS

2 MEDIUM CARROTS (240G)

1 LARGE GREEN APPLE (200G), UNPEELED

¼ RED CABBAGE (450G), SHREDDED FINELY

3 CUPS (480G) SHREDDED
BARBECUED CHICKEN

⅓ CUP CHOPPED FRESH CHIVES

100G (3 OUNCES) GORGONZOLA DOLCE
OR OTHER MILD BLUE CHEESE, CRUMBLED

DRESSSING

2 TABLESPOONS MAYONNAISE

1 TABLESPOON LEMON JUICE

1 TABLESPOON WATER

¼ TEASPOON CASTER SUGAR
(SUPERFINE SUGAR)

1 Make dressing.

2 Place nuts in a dry small frying pan over low heat, tossing frequently, for 2 minutes or until golden. Transfer to a large bowl.

3 Cut carrots and unpeeled apple into matchstick-sized pieces.

4 Add carrot and apple to large bowl with cabbage, chicken, chives and cheese; toss gently to combine.

5 Transfer slaw to a platter, drizzle with dressing; season with freshly ground black pepper.

DRESSING Whisk ingredients together in a small bowl; season to taste.

TIP You will need a barbecued chicken weighing about 900g (1¾ pounds).

nutritional count per serving *22.9g total fat (7.7g saturated fat); 1945kJ (465 cal); 14g carbohydrate; 46.6g protein; 7.4g fibre*

WRAP THE QUESADILLAS IN BAKING PAPER BEFORE YOU COOK THEM IN THE SANDWICH PRESS – THIS WILL HELP TO KEEP THE PRESS CLEAN. IF YOU DON'T HAVE A SANDWICH PRESS, PLACE THE QUESADILLAS ON BAKING-PAPER-LINED OVEN TRAYS AND BAKE AT 220°C/425°F FOR 15 MINUTES, SWAPPING TRAYS FROM TOP TO BOTTOM HALFWAY THROUGH COOKING TIME.

BEEF QUESADILLAS

1 Using a fork, mash avocado and juice in a small bowl. Season to taste.

2 Heat oil in a large frying pan over medium heat; cook beef, stirring, until browned. Add cumin; cook, stirring, 1 minute or until fragrant. Stir in beans, tomato and green onion. Remove pan from heat.

3 Divide beef mixture among four tortillas, then sprinkle with cheddar; top with remaining tortillas. Cook one at a time in a heated sandwich press, for 2 minutes or until cheddar is melted and tortillas are browned lightly.

4 Cut quesadillas into quarters; serve with avocado mixture, sour cream and lemon wedges.

SERVING SUGGESTION Serve with a green salad.

PREP + COOK TIME 25 MINUTES

SERVES 4

1 MEDIUM AVOCADO (250G), CHOPPED

1 TABLESPOON LEMON JUICE

1 TABLESPOON VEGETABLE OIL

500G (1 POUND) MINCED (GROUND) BEEF

2 TEASPOONS GROUND CUMIN

400G (12½ OUNCES) CANNED KIDNEY BEANS, DRAINED, RINSED

3 MEDIUM ROMA (EGG) TOMATOES (225G), CHOPPED FINELY

3 GREEN ONIONS (SCALLIONS), SLICED THINLY

8 X 19CM (7¾-INCH) FLOUR TORTILLAS

1 CUP (120G) GRATED CHEDDAR

¼ CUP (60G) SOUR CREAM

1 MEDIUM LEMON (140G), CUT INTO WEDGES

nutritional count per serving 50.4g total fat (21.4g saturated fat); 3329kJ (795 cal); 32.8g carbohydrate; 49.2g protein; 8.3g fibre

SANDWICHES

HAM & BASIL COLESLAW ROLLS

PREP TIME 10 MINUTES SERVES 2

Whisk 2 tablespoons 99% fat-free mayonnaise with 2 tablespoons skim-milk yoghurt in a medium bowl until combined. Mix in 1 cup finely shredded cabbage, ½ coarsely grated medium carrot, 1 thinly sliced shallot and 2 tablespoons torn fresh basil leaves. Season. Split 2 multigrain bread rolls in half; sandwich coleslaw and 125g (4 ounces) shaved light ham between rolls. Serve each roll with 1 large apple.

TIP You can use rare-roast beef or flaked hot smoked trout instead of the ham, if you prefer.

VIETNAMESE-STYLE VEGIE ROLL

PREP TIME 10 MINUTES SERVES 2

Peel 1 lebanese cucumber and ½ medium carrot into ribbons. Split 2 crusty long white bread rolls lengthways, without cutting all the way through. Spread the base of each roll with 2 tablespoons 99% fat-free mayonnaise; top rolls with 1 cup finely shredded iceberg lettuce, then carrot and cucumber ribbons. Drizzle with 2 tablespoons sweet chilli sauce; top with ⅓ cup firmly packed fresh coriander (cilantro) leaves. Season. Serve each roll with 1 large apple.

TIP If you want to make the rolls more substantial add a couple of slices of marinated tofu.

ROAST BEEF ON RYE

PREP TIME 10 MINUTES SERVES 2

Spread 1½ tablespoons horseradish cream over 2 slices rye bread then top each with 2 slices of rare roast beef. Divide 45g (1½ ounces) baby rocket (arugula) leaves and 2 tablespoons drained sun-dried tomato strips between sandwiches. Season. Top with another slice of rye bread. Serve with cornichons and 1 large apple each.

TIP Rye bread is a great choice for lunch as it is a low GI food, keeping you full for longer and therefore you're less likely to reach for a sugar fix in the afternoon.

PRAWN CLUB SANDWICH WITH CHIPS

PREP + COOK TIME 35 MINUTES SERVES 4

Preheat oven to 220°C/425°F. Cook 800g (1½ pounds) frozen potato chips according to packet directions. Meanwhile, thinly slice 2 medium tomatoes and separate leaves from 1 small green oak leaf lettuce. Heat 2 teaspoons olive oil in a large frying pan over high heat; cook 4 rindless bacon slices cut into three even pieces for 5 minutes or until crisp. Drain on paper towel. Toast 8 slices white sourdough bread until golden; spread toast with ½ cup (150g) mayonnaise. Sandwich lettuce, tomato, bacon and 500g (1 pound) shelled cooked tiger prawns (shrimp) between toast slices. Serve with chips.

TIP To make a quick cocktail sauce, add a couple of teaspoons of tomato sauce (ketchup) and chilli sauce or Tabasco to the mayonnaise.

LAMB FILLET SALAD WITH SPINACH PESTO DRESSING

PREP + COOK TIME 25 MINUTES

SERVES 4

8 LAMB FILLETS (550G)

1 CLOVE GARLIC, CRUSHED

1 TABLESPOON OLIVE OIL

1 LARGE ZUCCHINI (150G)

2 LARGE ROMA (EGG) TOMATOES (180G), QUARTERED

4 FLAT MUSHROOMS (320G)

350G (11 OUNCES) BABY ROCKET (ARUGULA) LEAVES

2 TABLESPOONS MARINATING OIL FROM GOAT'S CHEESE (BELOW)

½ CUP (100G) SOFT MARINATED GOAT'S CHEESE (SEE TIP)

SPINACH PESTO DRESSING

½ CUP (130G) READY-MADE SPINACH PESTO

¼ CUP (60ML) OLIVE OIL

1 Combine lamb, garlic and oil in a medium bowl.

2 Using a vegetable peeler or mandoline, thinly slice zucchini lengthways into ribbons.

3 Cook zucchini, tomato and mushrooms on a heated oiled chargrill plate (or barbecue or grill) until browned and just tender. Remove from heat; cover to keep warm.

4 Meanwhile, cook lamb on heated oiled chargrill plate for 4 minutes for each side or until cooked as desired. Remove from heat, cover; rest 5 minutes.

5 Make spinach pesto dressing.

6 Place vegetables in a large bowl with rocket and marinating oil; toss gently to combine. Season to taste.

7 Slice lamb. Divide vegetable mixture among bowls, top with lamb and crumbled cheese; drizzle with dressing.

SPINACH PESTO DRESSING Place ingredients in a small screw-top jar; shake well.

TIP The oil from the marinated goat's cheese adds an extra depth of flavour to this dish. The cheese we used was marinated in a mixture of olive oil, garlic, thyme and chilli.

nutritional count per serving *50.9g total fat (10g saturated fat); 2224kJ (536 cal); 6.9g carbohydrate; 11.7g protein; 3.8g fibre*

USE A TRADITIONAL BASIL PESTO
OR A SUN-DRIED TOMATO VARIETY
INSTEAD OF SPINACH, IF YOU PREFER.

BARBECUED CHILLI PRAWNS WITH GREEN MANGO SALAD

1 Combine chilli, rind, juice, char siu sauce, honey and oil in a large bowl; add prawns, toss to coat in marinade. Cover; refrigerate until required.

2 Make green mango salad.

3 Cook prawns on a heated oiled chargrill plate (or barbecue or grill) for 2 minutes each side or until prawns change colour and are cooked through.

4 Serve prawns with salad.

GREEN MANGO SALAD Place noodles in a medium heatproof bowl; cover with boiling water, stand 3 minutes or until noodles are tender. Drain. Cook coconut in a dry frying pan, stirring frequently, over medium heat, for 2 minutes or until browned lightly. Place noodles and coconut in a large bowl with remaining ingredients; toss gently to combine.

USE A MANDOLINE OR V-SLICER TO THINLY SHRED THE MANGO. ALTERNATIVELY, YOU CAN USE AN ASIAN-STYLE VEGETABLE PEELER, AVAILABLE FROM KITCHENWARE SHOPS, THAT WILL PEEL IN THIN STRIPS. GREEN MANGOES ARE AVAILABLE FROM ASIAN GROCERS AND SELECTED GREEN GROCERS.

PREP + COOK TIME 30 MINUTES

SERVES 4

1 FRESH LONG RED CHILLI, CHOPPED FINELY

1 TABLESPOON FINELY GRATED LIME RIND

1 TABLESPOON LIME JUICE

2 TABLESPOONS CHAR SIU SAUCE

1 TABLESPOON HONEY

2 TABLESPOONS OLIVE OIL

1KG (2 POUNDS) UNCOOKED KING PRAWNS (SHRIMP)

GREEN MANGO SALAD

200G (6½ OUNCES) BEAN THREAD VERMICELLI NOODLES

½ CUP (25G) FLAKED COCONUT

1 MEDIUM GREEN MANGO (350G), SHREDDED

1 FRESH LONG RED CHILLI, SLICED THINLY

⅓ CUP (50G) ROASTED CASHEWS

90G (3 OUNCES) BABY ROCKET (ARUGULA) LEAVES

1 CUP LOOSELY PACKED CORIANDER (CILANTRO) LEAVES

¼ CUP (60ML) OLIVE OIL

2 TABLESPOONS LIME JUICE

nutritional count per serving *34.2g total fat (8.3g saturated fat); 2360kJ (564 cal); 32.7g carbohydrate; 30.5g protein; 3.9g fibre*

QUINCE PASTE CAN BE FOUND IN THE CHEESE SECTION OF SUPERMARKETS OR DELIS. YOU CAN USE PLUM PASTE OR ORANGE MARMALADE INSTEAD IF YOU PREFER. YOU COULD ALSO USE HALVED GREEN OR RED GRAPES, OR SWEETENED DRIED CRANBERRIES INSTEAD OF THE POMEGRANATE SEEDS.

GRILLED LAMB SALAD

PREP + COOK TIME 25 MINUTES

SERVES 4

⅓ CUP (100G) QUINCE PASTE

1 TABLESPOON WATER

1 MEDIUM RED ONION (170G), SLICED THINLY

1 TEASPOON CASTER SUGAR (SUPERFINE SUGAR)

2 TABLESPOONS WHITE WINE VINEGAR

600G (1¼ POUNDS) LAMB BACKSTRAP

2 LEBANESE CUCUMBERS (260G), PEELED INTO RIBBONS

250G (8 OUNCES) HALOUMI, TORN

1 CUP FRESH CORIANDER (CILANTRO) LEAVES, TORN

100G (3 OUNCES) MESCLUN OR OTHER SALAD MIX

½ CUP (75G) POMEGRANATE SEEDS

LEMON DRESSING

⅓ CUP (80ML) EXTRA VIRGIN OLIVE OIL

¼ CUP (60ML) LEMON JUICE

1 Stir quince paste and the water in a small saucepan over medium heat until smooth and mixture is heated through.

2 Combine onion, sugar and vinegar in a large bowl.

3 Brush lamb with quince paste mixture. Cook lamb in a heated oiled chargrill pan (or barbecue or grill) 3 minutes each side for medium-rare or until browned and cooked to your liking. Remove from heat, cover; rest 10 minutes.

4 Meanwhile, make lemon dressing.

5 Drain most of the vinegar from onion mixture. Add cucumber, haloumi, coriander, mesclun and pomegranate seeds to the bowl with half the dressing; toss gently to combine.

6 Cut lamb into thin slices on a slight diagonal across the grain. Layer salad and lamb on a large platter; drizzle with remaining dressing.

LEMON DRESSING Whisk ingredients in a small jug until combined. Season to taste.

TIP Fresh pomegranate seeds can sometimes be found in the fridge section of supermarkets or good green grocers. If they're not available, cut a whole pomegranate in half crossways; hold it, cut-side down, in the palm of your hand over a bowl, then hit the outside firmly with a wooden spoon. The seeds should fall out easily; discard any white pith that falls out with them. Pomegranate seeds will keep in the fridge for up to a week.

nutritional count per serving *37.9g total fat (12.8g saturated fat); 2498kJ (596 cal); 14g carbohydrate; 48g protein; 4g fibre*

MOZZARELLA MADE FROM BUFFALO MILK IS WHITER IN COLOUR AND TANGIER IN TASTE THAN COW'S MILK MOZZARELLA. IF YOU PREFER, YOU CAN USE EITHER A LARGE BALL OF COW'S MILK MOZZARELLA (FIOR DI LATTE) OR SMALLER BALLS OF BOCCONCINI INSTEAD.

CHORIZO, TOMATO & ROCKET PASTA SALAD

1 Cook pasta in a large saucepan of boiling water until almost tender; drain.

2 Meanwhile, toast pine nuts in a dry medium frying pan, over high heat, stirring continuously, until golden. Remove from pan immediately.

3 Thinly slice 1 chorizo. Remove then discard casing from second chorizo; finely chop chorizo. Cook sliced and chopped chorizo in same frying pan over high heat, stirring until browned all over. Drain chorizo on paper towel; reserve chorizo oil in pan.

4 Make dressing.

5 Place pasta, nuts and chorizo in a large bowl with tomatoes, rocket and dressing; toss gently to combine. Serve pasta topped with cheese; drizzle with reserved chorizo oil.

DRESSING Whisk ingredients together in a small bowl. Season to taste.

TIP For extra flavour, cut half the tomatoes in half; squeeze the juices from the cut halves as you add them to the pasta.

PREP + COOK TIME 25 MINUTES

SERVES 4

375G (12 OUNCES) LINGUINE PASTA

¼ CUP (40G) PINE NUTS

2 CURED CHORIZO SAUSAGES (340G)

200G (6½ OUNCES) MINI GRAPE TOMATOES

100G (3 OUNCES) BABY ROCKET (ARUGULA) LEAVES

250G (8 OUNCES) BUFFALO MOZZARELLA CHEESE, TORN INTO BITE-SIZED PIECES

DRESSING

1 CLOVE GARLIC, CRUSHED

2 TABLESPOONS EXTRA VIRGIN OLIVE OIL

2 TABLESPOONS LEMON JUICE

nutritional count per serving *48.2g total fat (17.2g saturated fat); 3706kJ (885 cal); 73.5g carbohydrate; 37.7g protein; 2.2g fibre*

PEPPERED STEAK SANDWICH WITH GRILLED TOMATOES

PREP + COOK TIME 20 MINUTES

SERVES 4

2 TABLESPOONS OLIVE OIL

2 TEASPOONS CRACKED BLACK PEPPER

4 BEEF MINUTE STEAKS (400G)

250G (8 OUNCES) CHERRY TRUSS TOMATOES, CUT INTO FOUR CLUSTERS

8 SLICES SOURDOUGH BREAD (560G)

⅓ CUP (100G) AÏOLI

½ CUP (70G) CARAMELISED ONION RELISH

½ CUP LOOSELY PACKED TRIMMED WATERCRESS

1 Combine oil and pepper in a shallow dish; add steaks, turn to coat.

2 Heat an oiled chargrill pan (or barbecue or grill) over medium-high heat; cook steaks for 2 minutes each side or until cooked as desired. Remove from pan, cover; rest 5 minutes.

3 Cook tomato clusters in chargrill pan for 3 minutes or until softened. Remove from pan.

4 Toast bread slices in chargrill pan for 30 seconds each side. Spread aïoli onto half the toasted slices; top each with steak, onion relish and watercress, then remaining toasted bread slices. Serve sandwiches with tomato clusters.

TIP Aïoli is garlic mayonnaise, available from the condiment aisle in most supermarkets.

nutritional count per sandwich *34.4g total fat (6.7g saturated fat); 3149kJ (752 cal); 62.3g carbohydrate; 38.2g protein; 10.3g fibre*

HAVE A BOWL OF WATER HANDY TO DIP YOUR HANDS INTO WHILE SHAPING THE MEATBALLS AS THIS WILL HELP PREVENT THE MIXTURE FROM STICKING TO YOUR HANDS.

GREEK LAMB MEATBALLS WITH TOMATO & MINT SALAD

1 Combine lamb, fetta, garlic, breadcrumbs, egg, rind, cumin and oregano in a large bowl. Roll level tablespoons of mixture into balls.

2 Heat oil in a large frying pan over medium heat; cook meatballs, turning occasionally, 8 minutes or until browned and cooked through.

3 Meanwhile, make tomato and mint salad.

4 Serve meatballs with salad.

TOMATO & MINT SALAD Depending on their size, halve or thinly slice tomatoes. Place tomatoes in a large bowl with remaining ingredients; toss gently to combine.

PREP + COOK TIME 30 MINUTES

SERVES 4

500G (1 POUND) MINCED (GROUND) LAMB

100G (3 OUNCES) FETTA, CRUMBLED

2 CLOVES GARLIC, CRUSHED

½ CUP (50G) PACKAGED BREADCRUMBS

1 EGG

2 TEASPOONS FINELY GRATED LEMON RIND

2 TEASPOONS GROUND CUMIN

1 TEASPOON DRIED OREGANO

1 TABLESPOON OLIVE OIL

TOMATO & MINT SALAD

400G (12½ OUNCES) MIXED BABY TOMATOES

1 LEBANESE CUCUMBER (130G), CHOPPED COARSELY

½ SMALL RED ONION (50G), SLICED THINLY

½ CUP FRESH MINT LEAVES

1½ TABLESPOONS OLIVE OIL

1½ TABLESPOONS BALSAMIC VINEGAR

ALSO KNOWN AS TOMATO MEDLEY, MIXED BABY TOMATOES ARE SOLD IN A PREPACKED PUNNET FROM MOST SUPERMARKETS. THE MIX CONTAINS VARIETIES SUCH AS GRAPE, CHERRY AND ROMA TOMATOES IN RED AND YELLOW AS WELL AS THE DARK-COLOURED KUMATO.

nutritional count per serving *36.5g total fat (12.9g saturated fat); 2211 kJ (528 cal); 12.5g carbohydrate; 36g protein; 3.2g fibre*

SMOKED SALMON & ROCKET BRUSCHETTA

PREP TIME 20 MINUTES

SERVES 2

4 SLICES CIABATTA BREAD (140G)

1 CLOVE GARLIC, HALVED

100G (3 OUNCES) BABY ROCKET (ARUGULA) LEAVES

2 GREEN ONIONS (SCALLIONS), SLICED THINLY

1 SMALL BEETROOT (BEET) (100G), PEELED, CUT INTO MATCHSTICKS

2 TEASPOONS BALSAMIC GLAZE

40G (1½ OUNCES) REDUCED-FAT CHIVE AND ONION CREAM CHEESE

1 LEBANESE CUCUMBER (130G), CUT INTO RIBBONS

4 SLICES SMOKED SALMON (120G)

2 TEASPOONS FRESH DILL SPRIGS

1 Toast bread; rub one side of toasts with garlic.

2 Meanwhile, place half the rocket in a medium bowl with onion, beetroot and balsamic glaze; toss gently to combine. Season to taste.

3 Spread toasts with cream cheese; top with remaining rocket, cucumber and salmon. Sprinkle with dill.

4 Serve bruschetta with rocket salad.

nutritional count per serving *8.1g total fat (2.9g saturated fat); 1501kJ (359 cal); 42.1g carbohydrate; 26.1g protein; 5.4g fibre*

USE A VEGETABLE PEELER TO SLICE THE
CUCUMBER LENGTHWAYS INTO THIN RIBBONS.
USE DISPOSABLE GLOVES WHEN HANDLING
BEETROOT TO PREVENT STAINING YOUR FINGERS.
IF TAKING TO WORK, TOAST THE BREAD AT LUNCH
TIME JUST BEFORE YOU'RE READY TO ASSEMBLE.

MUSHROOM, TOMATO & GOAT'S CHEESE OMELETTES

1 Heat half the oil in a 20cm (8-inch) frying pan over medium-high heat; cook mushrooms, stirring occasionally, 8 minutes or until browned.

2 Add garlic, thyme and tomatoes; cook, stirring, 2 minutes or until tomatoes are just softened. Season to taste. Remove from pan; cover to keep warm. Wipe pan clean.

3 Lightly beat eggs and the water with a pinch of salt in a large bowl until combined.

4 Heat ½ teaspoon of the remaining oil in same pan over high heat. Add a quarter of the egg mixture, tilting the pan for it to cover base. Push egg mixture into the centre of the pan from one side with a lifter or spatula letting the uncooked egg run over the base. Repeat until egg is almost set. Top half the omelette with a quarter each of the mushroom mixture and cheese. Fold omelette over; slide out of pan onto a plate, folding in half again as it slides onto the plate.

5 Repeat step 4 with remaining oil, egg mixture, mushroom mixture and cheese. If you like, serve omelettes topped with extra thyme sprigs and freshly ground black pepper.

PREP + COOK TIME 25 MINUTES

SERVES 4

1 TABLESPOON EXTRA VIRGIN OLIVE OIL

400G (12½ OUNCES) MIXED MUSHROOMS, SLICED (SUCH AS BUTTON, SWISS BROWN, FLAT, ENOKI, SHIMEJI)

1 CLOVE GARLIC, CRUSHED

½ TEASPOON CHOPPED FRESH THYME LEAVES

200G (6½ OUNCES) GRAPE TOMATOES, HALVED

8 FREE-RANGE EGGS

⅓ CUP (80ML) WATER

100G (3 OUNCES) DRAINED MARINATED GOAT'S CHEESE, CRUMBLED

OMELETTES ARE BEST SERVED IMMEDIATELY, BUT CAN BE KEPT WARM IN A 150°C/300°F OVEN FOR A FEW MINUTES WHILE YOU COOK THE REMAINING OMELETTES.

nutritional count per serving *20.7g total fat (7.4g saturated fat); 1204kJ (287 cal); 3g carbohydrate; 21.5g protein; 2.4g fibre*

RADICCHIO AND WITLOF HAVE A BITTER FLAVOUR.
YOU CAN USE BABY COS (ROMAINE) LETTUCE IF
YOU PREFER. YOU COULD USE CHERRY TOMATOES
INSTEAD OF THE GRAPE TOMATOES.

LENTIL, GORGONZOLA & WITLOF SALAD

PREP + COOK TIME 30 MINUTES

SERVES 4

½ CUP (100G) FRENCH-STYLE
GREEN LENTILS

¾ CUP (75G) WALNUTS

½ CUP (125ML) SHERRY OR
RED WINE VINEGAR

½ CUP (125ML) EXTRA VIRGIN OLIVE OIL

1 SMALL RADICCHIO (150G),
LEAVES SEPARATED

2 LARGE WITLOF (BELGIAN ENDIVE) (250G),
LEAVES SEPARATED

180G (5½ OUNCES) GRAPE TOMATOES,
HALVED IF LARGE

1 CUP LOOSELY PACKED FRESH
FLAT-LEAF PARSLEY LEAVES

120G (4 OUNCES) GORGONZOLA OR
OTHER SOFT BLUE CHEESE

1 Cook lentils in a medium saucepan of boiling water 25 minutes or until lentils are tender; drain. Rinse under cold water; drain well.

2 Meanwhile, stir nuts in a small frying pan over medium heat until toasted lightly. Transfer to a chopping board, cool slightly; chop coarsely.

3 Whisk vinegar and oil in a large serving bowl; season to taste. Add radicchio, witlof, tomatoes, parsley and lentils; toss gently to combine.

4 Serve salad topped with nuts and crumbled gorgonzola.

TIP To save time, you can use canned brown lentils instead of the french-style green lentils.

nutritional count per serving *49.6g total fat (9.9g saturated fat); 2379kJ (568 cal); 9.9g carbohydrate; 13.2g protein; 11.1g fibre*

KUMARA & GOAT'S CHEESE JACKET POTATOES

1 Preheat oven to 200°C/400°F. Line an oven tray with foil.

2 Scrub kumara; pierce all over with a fork. Wrap separately in plastic wrap; cook in a microwave oven on HIGH (100%) for 8 minutes or until tender. Cool 5 minutes; remove and discard plastic wrap.

3 For each kumara, cut a 2cm (¾-inch) deep slit lengthways, from one end to the other. Using a tea towel, gently squeeze the base of the kumara to open the top. Scoop two thirds of the flesh into a small bowl.

4 Add egg and half the chives to kumara flesh; stir to combine, season. Spoon mixture into kumara; top with cheese. Place on oven tray.

5 Bake kumara for 5 minutes or until cheese is golden. Serve sprinkled with remaining chives.

SERVING SUGGESTION Serve with a baby spinach and shaved parmesan salad.

PREP + COOK TIME 25 MINUTES

SERVES 4

4 SMALL KUMARA (ORANGE SWEET POTATO) (1 KG)

2 EGGS, BEATEN LIGHTLY

⅔ CUP CHOPPED FRESH CHIVES

150G (4½ OUNCES) SOFT GOAT'S CHEESE, CRUMBLED

nutritional count per serving *10.5g total fat (6.1g saturated fat); 1285kJ (307 cal); 35.8g carbohydrate; 15.1g protein; 4.8g fibre*

FALAFEL WITH EGGPLANT PUREE & TOMATO SALSA

PREP + COOK TIME 30 MINUTES

SERVES 4

2 MEDIUM EGGPLANTS (460G)

450G (14½ OUNCES) PACKAGED READY-MADE FALAFEL

2 CLOVES GARLIC, QUARTERED

2 TABLESPOONS TAHINI

¾ CUP (210G) GREEK-STYLE YOGHURT

2 TABLESPOONS LEMON JUICE

250G (8 OUNCES) ROCKET (ARUGULA) LEAVES

2 TABLESPOONS OLIVE OIL

TOMATO SALSA

3 MEDIUM TOMATOES (450G), CHOPPED FINELY

¼ CUP FINELY CHOPPED FRESH MINT

2 TABLESPOONS FINELY CHOPPED FRESH FLAT-LEAF PARSLEY

1 Preheat oven to 200°C/400°F.

2 Cut eggplant in half lengthways. Using a small knife, cut a criss-cross pattern on the cut side. Cook eggplant, cut-side down, on a heated oiled chargrill plate (or grill pan or barbecue), for 8 minues or until tender and soft. Cool slightly.

3 Meanwhile, reheat falafel in oven according to directions on packet.

4 Using a spoon, scoop eggplant flesh from skin. Discard skin. Blend or process eggplant flesh with garlic, tahini, yoghurt and juice until almost smooth; season to taste.

5 Make tomato salsa.

6 Serve falafel with eggplant puree, rocket and salsa; drizzle with oil.

TOMATO SALSA Combine ingredients in a medium bowl; season to taste.

SERVING SUGGESTION Serve with grilled flat bread.

nutritional count per serving *35.7g total fat (5.5g saturated fat); 2309kJ (552 cal); 30.7g carbohydrate; 18.1g protein; 19.5g fibre*

FAST DINNERS

TO SPEED PREPARATION TIME, USE A FOOD PROCESSOR TO GRATE THE ONION, A VEGETABLE PEELER TO SLICE THE CUCUMBER INTO RIBBONS, AND PREPARED CRUSHED GINGER AVAILABLE IN TUBES FROM SUPERMARKETS. IF YOU USE BAMBOO SKEWERS, SOAK THEM IN A SHALLOW DISH OF BOILING WATER, THEN DRAIN IMMEDIATELY. THIS WILL PREVENT THEM FROM BURNING DURING COOKING

SATAY CHICKEN SKEWERS

PREP + COOK TIME 20 MINUTES

SERVES 4

12 CHICKEN TENDERLOINS (900G)

1 TEASPOON CURRY POWDER

½ TEASPOON ONION POWDER

½ TEASPOON GARLIC POWDER

¼ TEASPOON GROUND CUMIN

¼ TEASPOON GROUND CHILLI

2 TABLESPOONS PEANUT OIL

1 LARGE BROWN ONION (200G), GRATED

2 TEASPOONS CRUSHED GINGER

1 CUP (250ML) COCONUT CREAM

¾ CUP (210G) CRUNCHY PEANUT BUTTER

2 TABLESPOONS SWEET CHILLI SAUCE

2 TABLESPOONS LIGHT SOY SAUCE

¼ CUP (35G) CRUSHED ROASTED PEANUTS

450G (14½ OUNCES) PACKAGED WHITE MICROWAVE RICE

1 TELEGRAPH CUCUMBER (400G), SLICED INTO THIN RIBBONS

1 Heat an oiled chargrill plate (or grill pan or barbecue).

2 Combine chicken, spices and half the oil in a large bowl; season. Thread chicken onto 12 skewers; cook 3 minutes each side or until cooked through.

3 Meanwhile, heat remaining oil in a small saucepan; cook onion and ginger, stirring, for 1 minute or until onion softens. Add coconut cream, peanut butter, sauces and nuts; simmer, stirring, 1 minute.

4 Microwave rice according to packet directions.

5 Serve skewers with rice, peanut sauce and cucumber ribbons. If you like, top with fresh coriander (cilantro) leaves and lime wedges.

nutritional count per serving 56.2g total fat (18.9g saturated fat); 4146kJ (991 cal); 44.4g carbohydrate; 72.6g protein; 9.7g fibre

TANDOORI CHICKEN WITH POMEGRANATE RAITA

1 Preheat oven to 220°C/425°F. Bring a medium saucepan of water to the boil.

2 Meanwhile, combine tandoori paste and yoghurt with chicken in a large bowl. Season. Cook chicken on a heated oiled chargrill plate (or grill or barbecue) for 2 minutes each side or until golden. Transfer to a baking-paper-lined oven tray; cover with foil.

3 Bake chicken 20 minutes or until cooked through.

4 Meanwhile, add rice to boiling water; cook 12 minutes or until rice is tender. Drain; rinse under hot water.

5 Make pomegranate raita.

6 Serve chicken with rice and pomegranate raita.

POMEGRANATE RAITA Combine yoghurt, rind, juice and half the seeds in a small bowl. Before serving, sprinkle with remaining seeds.

PREP + COOK TIME 30 MINUTES

SERVES 4

¼ CUP (75G) TANDOORI PASTE
2 TABLESPOONS YOGHURT
4 SMALL CHICKEN MARYLANDS (1.2KG)
1½ CUPS (300G) JASMINE RICE

POMEGRANATE RAITA
1 CUP (280G) YOGHURT
2 TEASPOONS FINELY GRATED LIME RIND
1 TABLESPOON LIME JUICE
⅓ CUP POMEGRANATE SEEDS

FRESH POMEGRANATE SEEDS CAN SOMETIMES BE FOUND IN THE FRIDGE SECTION OF SUPERMARKETS OR GOOD GREEN GROCERS. IF THEY'RE NOT AVAILABLE, CUT A WHOLE POMEGRANATE IN HALF CROSSWAYS; HOLD IT, CUT-SIDE DOWN, IN THE PALM OF YOUR HAND OVER A BOWL, THEN HIT THE OUTSIDE FIRMLY WITH A WOODEN SPOON. THE SEEDS SHOULD FALL OUT EASILY; DISCARD ANY WHITE PITH THAT FALLS OUT WITH THEM. POMEGRANATE SEEDS WILL KEEP IN THE FRIDGE FOR UP TO A WEEK.

nutritional count per serving *18.4g total fat (6.7g saturated fat); 2849kJ (681 cal); 76.4g carbohydrate; 49.2g protein; 1.9g fibre*

FIVE-SPICE PORK CUTLETS WITH PLUM SAUCE

PREP + COOK TIME 20 MINUTES

SERVES 4

4 PORK CUTLETS (940G)

1 TABLESPOON CHINESE FIVE SPICE

2 TABLESPOONS PEANUT OIL

1 BUNCH CHOY SUM (400G)

450G (14½ OUNCES) PACKAGED WHITE MICROWAVE RICE

¼ TEASPOON DRIED CHILLI FLAKES

PLUM SAUCE

⅓ CUP (75G) FIRMLY PACKED BROWN SUGAR

½ CUP (125ML) WATER

6 DRAINED CANNED WHOLE PLUMS (250G)

1 TABLESPOON CHINESE COOKING WINE

1 CINNAMON STICK

2 STAR ANISE

2 TABLESPOONS FISH SAUCE

2 TEASPOONS MALT VINEGAR

1 Heat a large frying pan over medium-high heat. Combine pork, five spice and oil in a large bowl; season. Cook pork 3 minutes each side or until cooked through. Remove from heat, cover; rest 5 minutes.

2 Meanwhile, make plum sauce.

3 Microwave choy sum until just wilted.

4 Microwave rice according to directions on packet; sprinkle with chilli.

5 Serve pork with choy sum and rice; drizzle with plum sauce.

PLUM SAUCE Stir sugar and the water in a medium saucepan over low heat until sugar dissolves. Discard stones from plums; add plums to pan with wine, cinnamon and star anise. Bring to the boil. Reduce heat; simmer, covered, 6 minutes or until plums are pulpy. Remove and discard cinnamon stick. Stir in fish sauce and vinegar; season to taste.

TIP You can use fresh plums when in season.

nutritional count per serving *16.1g total fat (4.1g saturated fat); 2282kJ (545 cal); 58.6g carbohydrate; 37.9g protein; 5.1g fibre*

INCREASE THE AMOUNT OF CHILLI POWDER, IF YOU
WANT A LITTLE EXTRA HEAT. YOU COULD ALSO HEAT THE
TORTILLAS ON A CHARGRILL PLATE OR SANDWICH PRESS,
IF YOU LIKE; SPRAY THE TORTILLAS WITH A LITTLE OIL.

CHICKEN FAJITAS

1 Combine spices and half the oil with chicken in a large bowl; season.

2 Thinly slice capsicums and onion. Finely chop half the coriander.

3 Heat remaining oil in a large frying pan; cook capsicum and onion, stirring, over high heat, for 5 minutes or until soft. Add chopped coriander; transfer to a medium bowl, cover to keep warm.

4 Cook chicken in same pan, stirring, until browned and cooked through. Return capsicum mixture to pan with the water; cook, stirring, until hot. Season to taste.

5 Meanwhile, heat tortillas in microwave according to directions on the packet.

6 Serve chicken with tortillas, sour cream, lime wedges and remaining coriander.

PREP + COOK TIME 15 MINUTES

SERVES 4

½ TEASPOON GROUND CUMIN

½ TEASPOON GROUND CORIANDER

½ TEASPOON GROUND CHILLI

½ TEASPOON SMOKED PAPRIKA

2 TABLESPOONS OLIVE OIL

500G (1 POUND) CHICKEN BREAST STIR-FRY STRIPS

1 LARGE RED CAPSICUM (BELL PEPPER) (350G)

1 LARGE YELLOW CAPSICUM (BELL PEPPER) (350G)

1 MEDIUM RED ONION (170G)

½ CUP LOOSELY PACKED FRESH CORIANDER (CILANTRO) LEAVES

¼ CUP (60ML) WATER

12 X 19CM (7¾-INCH) FLOUR TORTILLAS

1 CUP (240G) SOUR CREAM

1 LIME (90G), CUT INTO WEDGES

nutritional count per serving *42.4g total fat (18.9g saturated fat); 3370kJ (805 cal); 62.6g carbohydrate; 41g protein; 5.4g fibre*

MAKE SURE TO RINSE THE CORIANDER ROOT WELL AS DIRT CAN BE TRAPPED IN IT. CHICKEN BREAST FILLETS CAN BE USED INSTEAD OF THE TURKEY, IF YOU LIKE. DRIED SWEETENED CRANBERRIES ARE SOLD AS 'CRAISINS' AND CAN BE FOUND IN THE BAKING AISLE OF SUPERMARKETS.

TURKEY PILAF

PREP + COOK TIME 25 MINUTES

SERVES 4

1 STALK FRESH CORIANDER (CILANTRO) WITH ROOT ATTACHED

1 TABLESPOON OLIVE OIL

600G (1¼ POUNDS) TURKEY BREAST FILLETS, SLICED THINLY

1 MEDIUM BROWN ONION (150G), SLICED THINLY

1 CLOVE GARLIC, SLICED THINLY

1 CINNAMON STICK

1 TEASPOON YELLOW MUSTARD SEEDS

1½ CUPS (300G) BASMATI RICE

1½ CUPS (375ML) WATER

1½ CUPS (375ML) CHICKEN STOCK

⅓ CUP (45G) DRIED SWEETENED CRANBERRIES

¼ CUP (35G) PISTACHIOS, ROASTED, CHOPPED COARSELY

½ CUP FRESH CORIANDER (CILANTRO) LEAVES, EXTRA

1 Remove leaves from coriander stalk; reserve. Finely chop root and stem.

2 Heat oil in a large saucepan over medium heat; cook turkey, in batches, until browned. Remove from pan.

3 Cook onion in same pan, stirring, until softened. Add garlic, coriander root and stem, cinnamon and mustard seeds; cook, stirring, until fragrant. Stir in rice, the water and stock; bring to the boil. Reduce heat; cook, covered, over low heat, 10 minutes or until water is absorbed.

4 Stir turkey and cranberries into pilaf; cook 5 minutes. Season to taste. Cover; stand 5 minutes.

5 Serve pilaf topped with nuts, and reserved and extra coriander leaves.

nutritional count per serving *10g total fat (1.4g saturated fat); 2335kJ (558 cal); 69.9g carbohydrate; 43.8g protein; 3.5g fibre*

DUKKAH IS AN EGYPTIAN SPICE BLEND MADE WITH ROASTED NUTS AND AROMATIC SPICES. IT IS AVAILABLE FROM MAJOR SUPERMARKETS AND DELICATESSENS.

DUKKAH-CRUSTED LAMB CUTLETS WITH CAULIFLOWER

1 Preheat grill (broiler).

2 Trim cauliflower; cut into 1.5cm (¾-inch) thick slices. Place on an oven tray; drizzle with half the oil, season. Place cauliflower under grill for 8 minutes, turning halfway through cooking time, or until tender. Scatter with nuts; grill further 20 seconds or until nuts are browned lightly. Remove from grill; sprinkle juice over cauliflower mixture.

3 Meanwhile, spray a large frying pan with cooking-oil; heat over medium-high heat.

4 Place dukkah in a shallow bowl. Combine pomegranate molasses with remaining oil; rub onto lamb, season. Press lamb firmly onto dukkah to coat both sides. Cook lamb in heated pan for 3 minutes each side or until cooked as desired.

5 Arrange lamb on cauliflower mixture, top with herbs; serve with baba ganoush, sprinkled with paprika.

SERVING SUGGESTION Serve with kumara crisps: heat oil in a large frying pan over high heat until hot. Using a vegetable peeler, slice kumara into thin strips. Shallow-fry kumara, in batches, in hot oil until crisp. Drain on paper towel.

PREP + COOK TIME 15 MINUTES

SERVES 4

1 SMALL CAULIFLOWER (1KG)

¼ CUP (60ML) OLIVE OIL

¼ CUP (20G) NATURAL SLICED ALMONDS

2 TEASPOONS LEMON JUICE

⅓ CUP (45G) DUKKAH

2 TABLESPOONS POMEGRANATE MOLASSES OR BALSAMIC GLAZE

12 FRENCH-TRIMMED LAMB CUTLETS (600G)

COOKING-OIL SPRAY

1 TABLESPOON FRESH FLAT-LEAF PARSLEY LEAVES

1 TABLESPOON FRESH MINT LEAVES

½ CUP (100G) READY-MADE BABA GANOUSH

¼ TEASPOON SMOKED PAPRIKA

nutritional count per serving *40.4g total fat (11g saturated fat); 2121kJ (507 cal); 8.9g carbohydrate; 23g protein; 6g fibre*

TO SAVE TIME, BUY PRE-CLEANED, BEARDED MUSSELS. IT'S A COOKING MYTH THAT UNOPENED MUSSELS SHOULD BE DISCARDED. IF YOU CAN PRY THEM OPEN, THEY ARE SAFE TO EAT. THE REASON THEY DON'T OPEN IS SIMPLY DUE TO HOW THE SHELL HAS FORMED.

GARLIC & CHILLI MUSSELS

PREP + COOK TIME 20 MINUTES

SERVES 4

60G (2 OUNCES) BUTTER, CHOPPED

3 CLOVES GARLIC, CHOPPED FINELY

1 FRESH LONG RED CHILLI, SLICED THINLY

⅓ CUP (80ML) DRY WHITE WINE

1KG (2 POUNDS) SMALL BLACK MUSSELS, SCRUBBED, BEARDED

⅓ CUP COARSELY CHOPPED FRESH FLAT-LEAF PARSLEY

1 Heat butter, garlic and chilli in a large saucepan, stirring, until fragrant.

2 Add wine to pan; bring to the boil. Add mussels; cover with a tight-fitting lid. Cook 5 minutes, shaking pan occasionally, or until mussels open. Stir in parsley; season to taste.

SERVING SUGGESTION Serve with crusty bread or a bowl of french fries.

nutritional count per serving *13.3g total fat (8.4g saturated fat); 702kJ (168 cal); 2.8g carbohydrate; 6.3g protein; 0.6g fibre*

RICOTTA & SPINACH AGNOLOTTI

1 Cook agnolotti in a large saucepan of boiling salted water until cooked through; drain.

2 Melt butter in same cleaned pan over medium heat; cook silver beet, covered, 5 minutes or until slightly wilted. Add cinnamon; cook, stirring, until fragrant.

3 Add soup to pan, bring to the boil; boil for 2 minutes. Add cream and agnolotti; stirring until well combined and heated through. Remove from heat. Stand 5 minutes before serving.

4 Serve agnolotti, topped with cheese slices; season with freshly ground black pepper.

TIPS We used agnolotti, a half-moon shaped filled pasta but you can use any vegetarian-style filled pasta you prefer. We used a white cheese from the Castello range, with a mild flavour. You could use brie or camembert.

PREP + COOK TIME 25 MINUTES

SERVES 6

625G (1¼ POUNDS) FRESH RICOTTA AND SPINACH AGNOLOTTI

50G (1½ OUNCES) BUTTER

500G (1 POUND) SILVER BEET (SWISS CHARD), TRIMMED, SHREDDED FINELY

1½ TEASPOONS GROUND CINNAMON

1KG (2 POUNDS) CANNED PUMPKIN SOUP

½ CUP (125ML) POURING CREAM

100G (3 OUNCES) WHITE MOULD CHEESE, SLICED

nutritional count per serving *31.3g total fat (19.6g saturated fat); 2465kJ (589 cal); 55.7g carbohydrate; 18.9g protein; 5.2g fibre*

SPICY RED BEANS WITH RICE

PREP + COOK TIME 30 MINUTES

SERVES 4

1½ CUPS (300G) BASMATI RICE

1¾ CUPS (430ML) WATER

1 TABLESPOON OLIVE OIL

1 MEDIUM BROWN ONION (150G), CHOPPED FINELY

3 CLOVES GARLIC, CRUSHED

1 STICK CELERY (150G), TRIMMED, CHOPPED COARSELY

1 MEDIUM RED CAPSICUM (BELL PEPPER) (200G), CHOPPED COARSELY

200G (6½ OUNCES) BUTTON MUSHROOMS, QUARTERED

200G (6½ OUNCES) SWISS BROWN MUSHROOMS

1 TABLESPOON MEXICAN CHILLI POWDER

400G (12½ OUNCES) CANNED KIDNEY BEANS, DRAINED, RINSED

1 CUP (250ML) WATER, EXTRA

1 CUP (250ML) TOMATO PUREE

½ CUP (140G) SOUR CREAM

3 GREEN ONIONS (SCALLIONS), SLICED THINLY

½ CUP FRESH CORIANDER (CILANTRO) SPRIGS

1 Rinse rice in a sieve under cold water until water runs clear; drain well. Place rice in a medium saucepan with the water; season. Cover; bring to the boil. Reduce heat to low; cook, 8 minutes or until water is absorbed.
2 Meanwhile, heat oil in a large saucepan over medium heat; cook onion, garlic, celery, capsicum and mushrooms, stirring, for 5 minutes or until softened. Add chilli powder; cook, stirring, 1 minute or until fragrant.
3 Add beans, the extra water and puree to pan; bring to the boil. Reduce heat to low; simmer, 15 minutes or until sauce thickens. Season to taste.
4 Divide rice and bean mixture among bowls. Serve topped with sour cream, green onion and coriander.

nutritional count per serving *20.1g total fat (9.6g saturated fat); 2462kJ (588 cal); 80.3g carbohydrate; 16.5g protein; 10.8g fibre*

CURRY LEMON CHICKEN BURGERS

1 Combine chicken, curry powder, green onion, rind and egg in a medium bowl; season.

2 Using damp hands, shape chicken mixture into four even-sized patties. Place on a baking-paper-lined oven tray. Cover; refrigerate 10 minutes.

3 Meanwhile, combine yoghurt and juice in a small bowl. Season.

4 Heat oil in a large frying pan over medium heat; cook patties, in batches, flattened slightly, for 3 minutes each side or until golden and cooked through.

5 Split bread rolls in half; spread bottom half of each roll with yoghurt mixture. Sandwich patty, eggplant and rocket between rolls.

SERVING SUGGESTION Serve with roasted potato wedges or chips.

PREP + COOK TIME 20 MINUTES

MAKES 4

500G (1 POUND) LEAN MINCED (GROUND) CHICKEN

1 TABLESPOON MILD CURRY POWDER

2 GREEN ONIONS (SCALLIONS), SLICED THINLY

2 TEASPOONS FINELY GRATED LEMON RIND

1 EGG

½ CUP (140G) GREEK-STYLE YOGHURT

1½ TABLESPOONS LEMON JUICE

2 TABLESPOONS OLIVE OIL

4 ROUND TURKISH BREAD ROLLS (660G)

1 CUP (160G) DRAINED MARINATED CHARGRILLED EGGPLANT, HALVED CROSSWAYS

80G (2½ OUNCES) BABY ROCKET (ARUGULA) LEAVES

nutritional count per burger 27.4g total fat (6.7g saturated fat); 3135kJ (749 cal); 79g carbohydrate; 42.8g protein; 6.9g fibre

IF YOU CAN'T FIND CHICKEN MINUTE STEAKS OR UNCRUMBED SCHNITZELS, CUT 4 CHICKEN BREAST FILLETS IN HALF HORIZONTALLY TO MAKE 8 PIECES. IF YOU PREFER YOU CAN MAKE A MUSTARD SAUCE FOR THE CHICKEN, REPLACE MARSALA WITH DRY WHITE WINE AND STIR 2 TEASPOONS WHOLEGRAIN MUSTARD INTO THE FINISHED SAUCE.

MARSALA CHICKEN WITH WHITE BEAN PUREE

PREP + COOK TIME 30 MINUTES

SERVES 4

1 TABLESPOON OLIVE OIL

8 X 90G (3-OUNCE) CHICKEN MINUTE STEAKS

⅔ CUP (160ML) MARSALA

¼ CUP (60ML) WATER

¼ CUP (60ML) POURING CREAM

WHITE BEAN PUREE

800G (1½ POUNDS) CANNED CANNELLINI BEANS, DRAINED, RINSED

¼ CUP (60ML) LEMON JUICE

1 CLOVE GARLIC

1 Heat oil in a large frying pan over high heat; cook chicken, in batches, for 2 minutes each side or until browned and cooked through. Remove from pan; rest, covered to keep warm.

2 Meanwhile, make white bean puree.

3 Add marsala and the water to same frying pan; cook, stirring, for 3 minutes or until liquid is reduced by half. Add cream; cook, stirring occasionally, for 2 minutes or until mixture is reduced and thickened. Season to taste.

4 Serve chicken and white bean puree with marsala sauce.

WHITE BEAN PUREE Blend or process ingredients until smooth. Transfer to a medium saucepan; cook puree until warmed through. Season to taste.

SERVING SUGGESTION Serve with steamed greens such as asparagus, beans and broccolini, or roasted truss tomatoes.

nutritional count per serving *13.4g total fat (5.3g saturated fat); 1878kJ (449 cal); 19.6g carbohydrate; 49.2g protein; 7.1g fibre*

RED TOFU CURRY

1 Heat oil in a medium saucepan over medium heat; cook onion, stirring, 3 minutes or until softened slightly.

2 Add curry paste, coconut milk, the water and carrots to pan, bring to a simmer; cook, stirring, 4 minutes. Add broccolini and tofu puffs; cook 2 minutes. Add snow peas; simmer, 1 minute or until just tender. Season to taste.

3 Serve curry topped with coriander.

SERVING SUGGESTION Serve with steamed jasmine rice.

PREP + COOK TIME 15 MINUTES

SERVES 4

1 TABLESPOON VEGETABLE OIL

1 MEDIUM RED ONION (170G), SLICED THINLY

⅓ CUP (100G) RED CURRY PASTE

1 CUP (250ML) COCONUT MILK

½ CUP (125ML) WATER

1 BUNCH BABY CARROTS (400G), TRIMMED

175G (5½ OUNCES) BROCCOLINI, TRIMMED

200G (6½ OUNCES) FRIED TOFU PUFFS, HALVED

100G (3 OUNCES) SNOW PEAS, TRIMMED

1 CUP LIGHTLY PACKED FRESH CORIANDER (CILANTRO) SPRIGS

FRIED TOFU PUFFS ARE CUBES OF FIRM TOFU THAT HAVE BEEN DEEP-FRIED SO THAT THEY PUFF UP. THEY ARE SOLD IN PACKETS AND ARE AVAILABLE IN THE REFRIGERATED SECTION OF ASIAN FOOD STORES.

nutritional count per serving *22.4g total fat (13g saturated fat); 1250kJ (298 cal); 13.1g carbohydrate; 11.6g protein; 11.5g fibre*

CHICKEN, FETTA & MUSHROOM PASTA

PREP + COOK TIME 25 MINUTES

SERVES 6

500G (1 POUND) SPIRAL PASTA

2 TABLESPOONS GARLIC BUTTER SPREAD

200G (6½ OUNCES) BUTTON MUSHROOMS, HALVED

2 GREEN ONIONS (SCALLIONS), SLICED THINLY

3 CUPS (480G) SHREDDED BARBECUED CHICKEN

200G (6½ OUNCES) DANISH FETTA, CRUMBLED

300ML POURING CREAM

2 TABLESPOONS COARSELY CHOPPED FRESH TARRAGON

2 GREEN ONIONS (SCALLIONS), EXTRA, SLICED THINLY

1 Cook pasta in a large saucepan of boiling salted water until almost tender. Drain, reserving 2 cups of the cooking liquid.

2 Melt butter in same cleaned pan; cook mushrooms, over medium heat, stirring until golden and tender.

3 Return pasta to pan; add green onion and chicken. Stir in fetta, cream, tarragon and reserved cooking liquid; cook, stirring until creamy and heated through. Season to taste.

4 Serve pasta topped with extra green onion.

TIPS You will need to buy a barbecued chicken weighing about 900g (1¾ pounds) for this recipe. Tarragon can be a bit tricky to find at some times of the year; if unavailable, use dill or flat-leaf parsley.

SERVING SUGGESTION Serve with a green bean and tomato salad.

nutritional count per serving *34.8g total fat (20.1g saturated fat); 2993kJ (715 cal); 60.4g carbohydrate; 37.8g protein; 3.3g fibre*

MOROCCAN LAMB CUTLETS WITH COUSCOUS SALAD

1 Preheat grill (broiler).

2 Combine ras el hanout and half the oil in a large bowl; add lamb, turn to coat in mixture.

3 Quarter capsicums; discard seeds and membrane. Place, skin-side up, on a foil-lined oven tray, drizzle with remaining oil. Place under hot grill for 15 minutes or until skin blisters and blackens. Cover capsicum with plastic wrap or paper, leave 5 minutes; peel away skin, then slice thinly.

4 Meanwhile, bring the water, butter and salt to the boil in a medium saucepan. Stir in couscous; cover, stand 5 minutes. Fluff with a fork.

5 Spoon hummus into a small serving bowl; sprinkle with a little extra ras el hanout.

6 Combine couscous, capsicum, preserved lemon and parsley in a large bowl.

7 Cook lamb on a heated oiled chargrill plate (or grill or barbecue) for 4 minutes each side or until cooked as desired.

8 Serve lamb with couscous salad and hummus.

TIP You can used store-bought chargrilled capsicum for this recipe, if you like.

PREP + COOK TIME 30 MINUTES

SERVES 4

2 TEASPOONS RAS EL HANOUT

⅓ CUP (80ML) OLIVE OIL

12 FRENCH-TRIMMED LAMB CUTLETS (600G)

1 MEDIUM GREEN CAPSICUM (BELL PEPPER) (200G)

1 MEDIUM YELLOW CAPSICUM (BELL PEPPER) (200G)

1 MEDIUM RED CAPSICUM (BELL PEPPER) (200G)

2 CUPS (500ML) WATER

30G (1 OUNCE) BUTTER

1 TEASPOON SEA SALT FLAKES

2 CUPS (400G) COUSCOUS

200G (6½ OUNCES) HUMMUS

1½ TABLESPOONS FINELY CHOPPED PRESERVED LEMON RIND

¼ CUP TORN FRESH FLAT-LEAF PARSLEY LEAVES

RAS EL HANOUT IS A BLEND OF MOROCCAN SPICES; 30 OR MORE SPICES CAN BE USED TO MAKE THE BLEND, WHICH INCLUDES CARDAMOM, MACE, NUTMEG, ANISE, CINNAMON, GINGER, PEPPER AND TURMERIC. YOU CAN USE A MOROCCAN SEASONING INSTEAD OR AN EQUAL MIX OF GROUND CUMIN AND GROUND CORIANDER.

nutritional count per serving *50.2g total fat (15.7g saturated fat); 3898kJ (931 cal); 81g carbohydrate; 33.3g protein; 12.2g fibre*

SAMBAL OELEK IS A CHILLI-BASED CONDIMENT AVAILABLE FROM THE ASIAN SECTION OF MAJOR SUPERMARKETS. IF UNAVAILABLE SUBSTITUTE 2 SMALL SEEDED RED CHILLIES, OR 1 FOR A LESS FIERY STIR-FRY.

LAMB, CHILLI & BLACK BEAN STIR-FRY

PREP + COOK TIME 30 MINUTES

SERVES 4

1 TABLESPOON PEANUT OIL

500G (1 POUND) LAMB BACKSTRAP, SLICED THINLY

300G (9½ OUNCES) BROCCOLI, CUT INTO FLORETS

300G (9½ OUNCES) GREEN BEANS, TRIMMED

⅔ CUP (160ML) WATER

300G (9½ OUNCES) SNOW PEAS, TRIMMED

½ CUP (125ML) BLACK BEAN SAUCE

6 GREEN ONIONS (SCALLIONS), CUT INTO 5CM (2-INCH) LENGTHS

3 TEASPOONS SAMBAL OELEK

1 Heat half the oil in a wok over high heat; stir-fry lamb, in batches, for 2 minutes or until browned all over. Remove from wok.

2 Heat remaining oil in wok; stir-fry broccoli, beans and half the water until tender. Return lamb to wok with snow peas, black bean sauce and the remaining water; stir-fry until snow peas are tender and lamb is heated through. Add onion and sambal oelek; stir-fry to combine. Season to taste.

SERVING SUGGESTION Serve with steamed jasmine rice.

nutritional count per serving *13.5g total fat (3.5g saturated fat); 1263kJ (302 cal); 8.9g carbohydrate; 33.3g protein; 5.8g fibre*

YOU CAN USE ANY SHORT PASTA YOU LIKE INSTEAD OF THE FARFALLE, ESPECIALLY SHORT TUBULAR TYPES, SUCH AS PENNE OR RIGATONI. COOK THE PASTA UNTIL IT'S 'FIRM TO THE TOOTH' OR, AS THE ITALIANS SAY, 'AL DENTE'.

LAMB FARFALLE WITH ROASTED VEGETABLES

1 Preheat oven to 180°C/350°F.

2 Place eggplant, zucchini, onion, tomatoes and garlic on a large oven tray; spray with cooking oil, season. Roast 15 minutes or until tender.

3 Meanwhile, cook pasta in a large saucepan of boiling salted water until almost tender; drain.

4 Combine lamb, spices and 1 tablespoon of the oil in a large bowl; turn to coat lamb in spices.

5 Cook lamb on a heated oiled chargrill plate (or grill or barbecue) for 4 minutes or until browned all over and cooked as desired. Remove from heat, cover; rest 5 minutes. Slice thickly.

6 Place pasta, roasted vegetables, lamb and remaining oil in a large bowl with remaining ingredients; toss gently to combine. Season to taste.

PREP + COOK TIME 30 MINUTES

SERVES 6

1 MEDIUM EGGPLANT (300G), CHOPPED

1 LARGE ZUCCHINI (150G), CHOPPED

1 MEDIUM RED ONION (170G), SLICED THICKLY

250G (8 OUNCES) CHERRY TOMATOES, HALVED

2 CLOVES GARLIC, CRUSHED

COOKING-OIL SPRAY

375G (12 OUNCES) FARFALLE (BOWTIE) PASTA

600G (1¼ POUNDS) LAMB BACKSTRAPS

1 TEASPOON GROUND CORIANDER

1 TEASPOON GROUND CUMIN

¼ CUP (60ML) OLIVE OIL

⅓ CUP (80ML) LEMON JUICE

1 CUP FIRMLY PACKED FRESH MINT LEAVES

50G (1½ OUNCES) BABY SPINACH LEAVES

⅓ CUP (50G) TOASTED PINE NUTS

nutritional count per serving *22.4g total fat (4g saturated fat); 2254kJ (539 cal); 49.3g carbohydrate; 32g protein; 5.8g fibre*

QUICHES

CARAMELISED ONION & GOAT'S CHEESE QUICHES

PREP + COOK TIME 40 MINUTES MAKES 12

Preheat oven to 180°C/350°F. Heat 1 tablespoon olive oil and 20g (¾ ounce) butter in a medium frying pan over medium-high heat. Cook 2 large (400g) halved and thinly sliced onions with 1 teaspoon salt and 1 teaspoon brown sugar, stirring for 5 minutes or until onion starts to collapse. Reduce heat to medium; cook, covered, for a further 10 minutes, stirring occasionally or until caramelised. Remove from heat; stir in 2 teaspoons lemon thyme leaves. Whisk 2 eggs with 1 tablespoon milk in a medium jug; season. Grease a 12-hole (2-tablespoon/40ml) flat-based patty pan. Using a 7cm (3-inch) cutter, cut 12 rounds from 2 sheets of shortcrust pastry; press rounds into pan holes. Spoon onion mixture into pastry cases, top with egg mixture, then 60g (2 ounces) crumbled soft goat's cheese. Bake 25 minutes or until quiches are set and pastry is browned lightly. Serve warm.

TIP You can use fetta instead of goat's cheese, if you prefer.

MINI CHICKEN & ASPARAGUS QUICHES

PREP + COOK TIME 40 MINUTES MAKES 12

Preheat oven to 180°C/350°F. Whisk 3 eggs with 1 tablespoon milk in a medium jug; season. Grease a 12-hole (2-tablespoon/40ml) flat-based patty pan. Using a 7cm (3-inch) cutter, cut 12 rounds from 2 sheets of shortcrust pastry; press rounds into pan holes. Divide 5 (75g) chopped asparagus spears, 125g (4 ounces) finely shredded barbecued chicken and 2 tablespoons finely chopped fresh chives among pastry cases. Top with egg mixture; sprinkle with ¼ cup (20g) finely grated parmesan. Bake 25 minutes or until quiches are set and pastry is browned lightly. Serve warm.

TIP You could use 75g (2½ ounces) frozen peas instead of the asparagus and serve topped with a little crumbled ricotta.

MINI BLUE CHEESE QUICHES

PREP + COOK TIME 40 MINUTES MAKES 12

Preheat oven to 180°C/350°F. Whisk 2 eggs with 1 tablespoon milk in a medium jug; season. Grease a 12-hole (2-tablespoon/40ml) flat-based patty pan. Using a 7cm (3-inch) cutter, cut 12 rounds from 2 sheets of shortcrust pastry; press rounds into pan holes. Divide 150g (5 ounces) crumbled soft blue cheese and 1 tablespoon chopped fresh flat-leaf parsley among pastry cases. Top with egg mixture. Bake 25 minutes or until quiches are set and pastry is browned lightly. Top with extra parsley.

TIP If you are not a fan of blue cheese, you can use another strong-flavoured cheese, such as vintage cheddar or a washed rind cheese instead.

MINI HAM & CORN QUICHES

PREP + COOK TIME 40 MINUTES MAKES 12

Preheat oven to 180°C/350°F. Whisk 2 eggs with 1 tablespoon pouring cream in a medium jug; season. Grease a 12-hole (2-tablespoon/40ml) flat-based patty pan. Using a 7cm (3-inch) cutter, cut 12 rounds from 2 sheets of shortcrust pastry; press rounds into pan holes. Divide 90g (3 ounces) coarsely chopped leg ham and 310g (10 ounces) drained canned corn kernels between pastry cases. Top with egg mixture. Bake 25 minutes or until quiches are set and pastry is browned lightly. Meanwhile cook 2 slices prosciutto in a dry frying pan over medium heat, for 1 minute each side or until crisp. Crumble prosciutto on quiches.

CAULIFLOWER & CHEESE PASTA BAKE

PREP + COOK TIME 25 MINUTES

SERVES 4

250G (8 OUNCES) SPIRAL PASTA

30G (1 OUNCE) BUTTER

2 TABLESPOONS PLAIN (ALL-PURPOSE) FLOUR

2 CUPS (500ML) MILK

1½ CUPS (150G) COARSELY GRATED MOZZARELLA

2 TABLESPOONS COARSELY CHOPPED FRESH FLAT-LEAF PARSLEY

500G (1 POUND) FROZEN CAULIFLOWER FLORETS

1 EGG, BEATEN LIGHTLY

¼ CUP (20G) PANKO (JAPANESE) BREADCRUMBS

½ TEASPOON GROUND NUTMEG

1 Preheat grill (broiler). Oil a 2-litre (8-cup) ovenproof dish.

2 Cook pasta in a large saucepan of boiling water until almost tender; drain.

3 Meanwhile, to make cheese sauce, melt butter in a medium saucepan over medium heat, add flour; cook, stirring, until bubbling. Gradually stir in milk; cook, stirring, until mixture boils and thickens. Remove from heat; stir in 1 cup of the cheese, and the parsley.

4 Combine pasta, cheese sauce and cauliflower in a large bowl; stir in egg. Spoon mixture into dish, top with combined breadcrumbs and remaining cheese; sprinkle with nutmeg.

5 Place dish under hot grill for 10 minutes or until top is golden.

SERVING SUGGESTION Serve with a green leaf and mixed herb salad.

nutritional count per serving *22g total fat (12.9g saturated fat); 2361kJ (564 cal); 59.8g carbohydrate; 27.7g protein; 4g fibre*

CREAMY BEEF & MUSHROOM RIGATONI

1 Cook pasta in a large saucepan of boiling water until almost tender; drain well.

2 Meanwhile, coat beef in flour; shake off excess flour. Heat oil in a large saucepan over high heat; cook beef, in batches, until browned. Remove from pan; cover to keep warm.

3 Melt butter in same pan; cook shallots, garlic and mushrooms, stirring occasionally, until softened. Add brandy; cook, stirring, 30 seconds.

4 Add stock to pan; bring to the boil. Reduce heat; simmer, covered, 5 minutes. Return beef to pan with sour cream; stir until smooth. Remove from heat; season to taste. Add pasta and parsley; stir until combined.

5 Serve pasta sprinkled with parmesan and extra parsley.

TIP To save even more time, you can use beef stir-fry strips.

PREP + COOK TIME 30 MINUTES

SERVES 6

500G (1 POUND) RIGATONI PASTA

600G (1¼-POUND) PIECE BEEF FILLET, SLICED THINLY

¼ CUP (35G) PLAIN (ALL-PURPOSE) FLOUR

2 TABLESPOONS OLIVE OIL

20G (¾ OUNCE) BUTTER

4 SHALLOTS (100G), SLICED THINLY

2 CLOVES GARLIC, CRUSHED

375G (12 OUNCES) BUTTON MUSHROOMS, QUARTERED

⅓ CUP (80ML) BRANDY

2 CUPS (500ML) BEEF STOCK

1¼ CUPS (300G) SOUR CREAM

¼ CUP COARSELY CHOPPED FRESH FLAT-LEAF PARSLEY

¼ CUP (20G) FINELY GRATED PARMESAN

2 TABLESPOONS TORN FRESH FLAT-LEAF PARSLEY LEAVES, EXTRA

nutritional count per serving *48.9g total fat (23.6g saturated fat); 3945kJ (943 cal); 69.1g carbohydrate; 51.4g protein; 4.1g fibre*

THAI SPICY BEEF & NOODLE STIR-FRY

PREP + COOK TIME 30 MINUTES

SERVES 4

200G (6½ OUNCES) DRIED RICE NOODLES

1 TABLESPOON PEANUT OIL

500G (1 POUND) RUMP STEAK, SLICED THINLY

3 CLOVES GARLIC, CRUSHED

2 FRESH SMALL RED CHILLIES, CHOPPED FINELY

2 TABLESPOONS FISH SAUCE

2 TABLESPOONS DARK SOY SAUCE

1 TABLESPOON BROWN SUGAR

4 KAFFIR LIME LEAVES, SHREDDED

3 MEDIUM TOMATOES (450G), CHOPPED FINELY

¼ CUP FRESH CORIANDER (CILANTRO) LEAVES

1 Cook noodles according to directions on packet; drain.

2 Heat half the oil in a wok over high heat; stir-fry beef, in batches, until browned. Remove from wok; cover to keep warm.

3 Heat remaining oil in wok; stir-fry garlic and chilli until fragrant. Add sauces, sugar and lime leaves; stir-fry until combined.

4 Return beef to wok with noodles and tomato; stir-fry until tomato starts to soften and is heated through. Serve stir-fry topped with coriander.

YOU CAN MAKE THIS STIR-FRY WITH 500G (1 POUND) CHICKEN BREAST FILLETS, CUT INTO THIN STRIPS, INSTEAD OF THE BEEF IF YOU PREFER. TO INCREASE THE VEGIE CONTENT, ADD EITHER 100G (3 OUNCES) SNOW PEAS, TRIMMED OR 1 BUNCH (400G) CHOY SUM, CHOPPED, AT THE END OF STEP 3 AND STIR-FRY FOR 2 MINUTES OR UNTIL VEGIES ARE TENDER.

nutritional count per serving *16.6g total fat (5.3g saturated fat); 1692kJ (404 cal); 16.7g carbohydrate; 45.3g protein; 2.8g fibre*

PORK & ROSEMARY MEATBALLS WITH PASTA

1 Combine pork, half the onion, half the garlic, the breadcrumbs, egg and rosemary in a large bowl. Using damp hands, roll heaped tablespoons of mixture into balls.

2 Heat oil in a large saucepan over medium heat; cook remaining onion and garlic, stirring, until onion softens. Stir in paste; cook, stirring, 2 minutes. Add wine, pasta sauce and the water; bring to the boil.

3 Carefully drop the meatballs into the sauce; simmer 10 minutes or until meatballs are cooked through.

4 Meanwhile, just before the meatballs are cooked, cook pasta in a large saucepan of boiling water until almost tender; drain. (See tip.)

5 Serve pasta topped with meatballs, scatter with cheese.

PREP + COOK TIME 30 MINUTES

SERVES 4

500G (1 POUND) MINCED (GROUND) PORK

1 LARGE BROWN ONION (200G), CHOPPED FINELY

2 CLOVES GARLIC, CRUSHED

¼ CUP (15G) STALE BREADCRUMBS

1 EGG, BEATEN LIGHTLY

1½ TABLESPOONS COARSELY CHOPPED FRESH ROSEMARY

1 TABLESPOON OLIVE OIL

1 TABLESPOON TOMATO PASTE

½ CUP (125ML) DRY RED WINE

700G (1½ POUNDS) BOTTLED TOMATO PASTA SAUCE

1 CUP (250ML) WATER

375G (12 OUNCES) ANGEL HAIR PASTA

⅓ CUP (25G) FINELY GRATED PARMESAN

FRESH ANGEL HAIR PASTA WILL COOK IN SECONDS, AND THE DRIED PASTA IN A COUPLE OF MINUTES; IT IS USUALLY READY PRETTY MUCH AS SOON AS THE WATER RETURNS TO THE BOIL. UNCOOKED MEATBALLS CAN BE FROZEN FOR UP TO 3 MONTHS; PLACE THEM IN AN AIRTIGHT CONTAINER, SEPARATING THE LAYERS WITH BAKING PAPER TO PREVENT THEM STICKING TOGETHER.

nutritional count per serving *21.6g total fat (7.2g saturated fat); 3156kJ (754 cal); 85.5g carbohydrate; 46.4g protein; 1.3g fibre*

TALEGGIO, PROSCIUTTO & ROCKET PIZZA

PREP + COOK TIME 25 MINUTES

SERVES 4

1 LARGE RED ONION (300G), CUT INTO THIN WEDGES

1½ TABLESPOONS BALSAMIC VINEGAR

2 X 150G (4½-OUNCE) PIZZA BASES

½ CUP (130G) BOTTLED TOMATO AND BASIL PASTA SAUCE

½ CUP (50G) GRATED MOZZARELLA

½ CUP (100G) DRAINED ROASTED CAPSICUM (BELL PEPPER) STRIPS

6 SLICES PROSCIUTTO (90G), TORN ROUGHLY

150G (4½ OUNCES) TALEGGIO CHEESE, TORN

50G (1½ OUNCES) BABY ROCKET (ARUGULA) LEAVES

1 Preheat oven to 240°C/475°F.

2 Place onion on a baking-paper-lined oven tray; drizzle with vinegar. Bake 15 minutes or until onion is tender.

3 Meanwhile, place pizza bases on two lightly oiled oven trays; spread with pasta sauce, then top with mozzarella, capsicum, prosciutto and taleggio. Bake 12 minutes or until cheese melts and bases are crisp.

4 Combine rocket and baked onion in a medium bowl.

5 Cut pizzas into wedges; top with rocket mixture.

nutritional count per serving *17g total fat (8.8g saturated fat); 1850kJ (442 cal); 42.2g carbohydrate; 27g protein; 5.1g fibre*

TALEGGIO CHEESE IS A WASHED RIND ITALIAN CHEESE WITH A STRONG AROMA, BUT A COMPARATIVELY MILD TASTE. IT IS AVAILABLE FROM DELICATESSENS AND ITALIAN GROCERS. IF NOT AVAILABLE, USE FRESH MOZZARELLA OR FONTINA INSTEAD.

SALMON PIES

1 Preheat oven to 180°C/350°F. Oil a large oven tray; line with baking paper.

2 Place pastry sheets on a clean flat surface. Place one salmon fillet in the centre of each pastry sheet; season. Top salmon with green onion, dill and capers. Brush pastry edges with a little egg.

3 Working with one pastry sheet at a time, fold opposite sides of the pastry over the salmon. Fold other sides over to completely enclose salmon and form a parcel. Repeat with remaining pastry.

4 Place parcels, seam-side down, on oven tray. Using a sharp knife, score three diagonal lines across the top of each parcel (without cutting through pastry). Brush top of pastry with egg.

5 Bake parcels 15 minutes or until golden.

SERVING SUGGESTION Serve with a tomato and herb salad.

PREP + COOK TIME 25 MINUTES

MAKES 4

4 SHEETS PUFF PASTRY

4 X 220G (7-OUNCE) SKINLESS SALMON FILLETS

4 GREEN ONIONS (SCALLIONS), SLICED THINLY

1 TABLESPOON FINELY CHOPPED FRESH DILL

1 TABLESPOON BABY CAPERS

1 EGG, BEATEN LIGHTLY

nutritional count per pie *69.8g total fat (32.2g saturated fat); 5043kJ (1204 cal); 76.8g carbohydrate; 66.8g protein; 3.1g fibre*

99

STORE COOLED FRITTATA, COVERED, IN THE REFRIGERATOR FOR UP TO 2 DAYS. YOU CAN ALSO START COOKING THIS FRITTATA IN A NON-STICK OVENPROOF FRYING PAN ON THE STOVE TOP AND FINISH IT UNDER THE GRILL (BROILER). THE FRITTATA CAN BE EATEN WARM OR AT ROOM TEMPERATURE.

ASPARAGUS & FETTA FRITTATA

PREP + COOK TIME 35 MINUTES (+ COOLING)

SERVES 4

170G (5½ OUNCES) ASPARAGUS, TRIMMED, CHOPPED COARSELY

2 SMALL ZUCCHINI (180G), SLICED THINLY LENGTHWAYS

1 CUP (120G) FROZEN PEAS

8 EGGS

½ CUP (125ML) POURING CREAM

½ CUP LIGHTLY PACKED FRESH MINT LEAVES, TORN

150G (4½ OUNCES) FETTA, CRUMBLED

1 Preheat oven to 180°C/350°F. Oil a 20cm x 30cm (8-inch x 12-inch) rectangular pan; line base with baking paper, extending the paper 5cm (2 inches) over the long sides.

2 Place asparagus, zucchini and peas in a small saucepan of boiling water. Return to the boil; drain immediately, transfer to a bowl of iced water until cold. Drain well, then pat dry with paper towel.

3 Whisk eggs and cream in a large jug until combined. Add mint; season.

4 Place fetta and vegetables in pan; pour over egg mixture.

5 Bake frittata for 25 minutes or until set. Cool before cutting into slices.

nutritional count per serving *33.1g total fat (17.9g saturated fat); 1737kJ (415 cal); 5g carbohydrate; 23.7g protein; 3.3g fibre*

TUNA MACARONI

1 Preheat oven to 200°C/400°F. Oil six 1½-cup (375ml) ovenproof dishes.

2 Cook pasta in a large saucepan of boiling water until almost tender; drain.

3 Coarsely chop caspicum, then combine with pasta, tuna, asparagus and sauce in a large bowl; season to taste. Spoon mixture into dishes. Sprinkle with combined cheese and breadcrumbs.

4 Bake 10 minutes or until browned and heated through. Serve topped with parsley.

SERVING SUGGESTION Serve with a green salad.

PREP + COOK TIME 25 MINUTES

SERVES 4

150G (8 OUNCES) MACARONI

2 X 260G (8½ OUNCES) BOTTLED ROASTED RED CAPSICUM (BELL PEPPER) STRIPS IN OIL, DRAINED

425G (13½ OUNCES) CANNED TUNA IN SPRING WATER, DRAINED

170G (5½ OUNCES) ASPARAGUS, CHOPPED COARSELY

2¼ CUPS (540G) BOTTLED TUNA PASTA BAKE SAUCE

1½ CUPS (180G) COARSELY GRATED CHEDDAR

1 CUP (75G) PANKO (JAPANESE) BREADCRUMBS

2 TABLESPOONS TORN FRESH FLAT-LEAF PARSLEY

BE SURE TO CHOP CAPSICUM AND ASPARAGUS INTO FORK-FRIENDLY PIECES. YOU CAN USE ANY COMMERCIALLY-MADE WHITE SAUCE INSTEAD OF THE TUNA PASTA BAKE SAUCE.

nutritional count per serving *39.3g total fat (14.8g saturated fat); 3322kJ (794 cal); 58.3g carbohydrate; 49.6g protein; 3.2g fibre*

YOU COULD ALSO MAKE THE RECIPE WITH 4 CHICKEN
BREASTS INSTEAD OF VEAL CUTLETS, COOKING THEM
FOR ABOUT THE SAME AMOUNT OF TIME.

PROSCIUTTO-WRAPPED VEAL CUTLETS WITH TRUSS TOMATOES

PREP + COOK TIME 20 MINUTES

SERVES 4

2 TABLESPOONS DIJON MUSTARD

4 VEAL CUTLETS (1KG)

8 FRESH SAGE LEAVES

4 SLICES PROSCIUTTO (60G)

500G (1 POUND) TRUSS CHERRY TOMATOES

1½ TABLESPOONS OLIVE OIL

¼ CUP (60ML) BALSAMIC VINEGAR

¾ CUP (180ML) CHICKEN STOCK

1 Preheat oven to 200°C/400°F.

2 Spread mustard on one side of each veal cutlet; top each with 2 sage leaves. Wrap a slice of prosciutto around each cutlet; secure with a toothpick.

3 Place tomatoes on a baking-paper-lined oven tray. Drizzle with 2 teaspoons of the oil; season. Roast for 12 minutes or until skins start to split.

4 Meanwhile, heat remaining oil in a large frying pan over medium heat; cook veal for 5 minutes each side or until browned and cooked through. Remove from pan, cover; rest 5 minutes.

5 Add vinegar to same pan; simmer for 2 minutes or until syrupy. Stir in stock; simmer for 3 minutes or until liquid is reduced by half. Serve veal with tomatoes; drizzle with sauce.

SERVING SUGGESTION Serve with mashed potato.

nutritional count per serving *13.6g total fat (3.8g saturated fat); 1459kJ (348 cal); 3.7g carbohydrate; 51g protein; 2g fibre*

FAST DESSERTS

YOU WON'T NEED TO USE THE WHOLE PANETTONE FOR THIS RECIPE. LEFT OVER PANETTONE IS DELICIOUS TOASTED OR USED IN A TRIFLE. PANDORO, ANOTHER ITALIAN CHRISTMAS BREAD, BUT WITHOUT THE DRIED FRUIT, WOULD ALSO WORK WELL. WHEN CUT CROSSWAYS, PANDORO SLICES RESEMBLE A STAR SHAPE (SEE PREVIOUS PAGE). IF PANETTONE AND PANDORO ARE NOT AVAILABLE, YOU CAN SPREAD THE ALMOND MIXTURE ONTO SLICES OF SOURDOUGH OR BRIOCHE.

ALMOND PANETTONE WITH HONEY GRILLED PEACHES

PREP + COOK TIME 35 MINUTES

SERVES 8

8 MEDIUM PEACHES (1.2KG), HALVED, STONES REMOVED

½ CUP (175G) HONEY, WARMED

200G (6½ OUNCES) RASPBERRIES

100G (3 OUNCES) BUTTER

½ CUP (110G) CASTER SUGAR (SUPERFINE SUGAR)

2 EGGS

½ TEASPOON GROUND CINNAMON

1 CUP (120G) GROUND ALMONDS

2 TABLESPOONS ALMOND-FLAVOURED LIQUEUR

750G (1½-POUND) PANETTONE

½ CUP (40G) FLAKED ALMONDS

1 CUP (240G) FRESH RICOTTA

1 Preheat grill (broiler) to high. Preheat oven to 180°C/350°F.

2 Place peach halves, cut-side up, on a greased oven tray. Drizzle with honey and scatter with raspberries. Place under the grill for 8 minutes or until peaches are beginning to brown around the edges.

3 Meanwhile, to make almond mixture, beat butter and sugar in a small bowl with an electric mixer until light and fluffy. Beat in eggs. Stir in cinnamon, ground almonds and liqueur.

4 Cut panettone crossways into four 1.5cm (¾-inch) thick rounds; cut rounds into quarters. Spread slices with almond mixture, top with almonds; place on two baking-paper-lined oven trays. Bake 20 minutes or until golden.

5 Serve almond panettone with peaches and ricotta.

nutritional count per serving *36.5g total fat (14.3g saturated fat); 3340kJ (798 cal); 94.5g carbohydrate; 18.3g protein; 6.3g fibre*

APPLE & RASPBERRY CRUMBLES

1 Preheat oven to 220°C/425°F.

2 Cook apples, rind, juice and sugar in a large frying pan until apples begin to caramelise. Stir in mixed spice, the water and raspberries. Spoon mixture into four 1-cup (250ml) shallow ovenproof dishes.

3 Crumble biscuits into a small bowl. Rub in butter until mixture clumps slightly; stir in almonds. Sprinkle crumb mixture on fruit. Place dishes on an oven tray.

4 Bake for 10 minutes or until crumbles are heated through.

TIP You could use granny smith apples in this recipe, they will give a slightly tart flavour.

PREP + COOK TIME 35 MINUTES

SERVES 4

4 MEDIUM APPLES (600G), PEELED, CHOPPED COARSELY

2 TEASPOONS FINELY GRATED LEMON RIND

¼ CUP (60ML) LEMON JUICE

¼ CUP (55G) FIRMLY PACKED BROWN SUGAR

2 TEASPOONS MIXED SPICE

2 TABLESPOONS WATER

500G (1 POUND) FROZEN OR FRESH RASPBERRIES

125G (4 OUNCES) SCOTCH FINGER BISCUITS

20G (¾ OUNCE) BUTTER

20G (¾ OUNCE) NATURAL ALMOND FLAKES

nutritional count per serving *14g total fat (6.8g saturated fat); 1670kJ (404 cal); 58g carbohydrate; 5g protein; 10.4g fibre*

GLAZED FIG BRUSCHETTA

PREP + COOK TIME 10 MINUTES

SERVES 4

6 MEDIUM GREEN OR PURPLE FIGS (360G), HALVED

2 TABLESPOONS HONEY

1 TABLESPOON COLD WATER

⅔ CUP (160ML) THICKENED (HEAVY) CREAM

1 TABLESPOON ICING SUGAR (CONFECTIONERS' SUGAR)

⅓ CUP (85G) MASCARPONE

4 THICK SLICES BRIOCHE (150G), TOASTED

1 Drizzle cut-sides of figs with honey. Place figs, cut-side down, in a heated large non-stick frying pan; cook until figs are warmed through. Add the water to pan; remove from heat.

2 Meanwhile, beat cream and sifted icing sugar in a small bowl with an electric mixer until soft peaks form; beat in mascarpone.

3 Spread each brioche with mascarpone mixture; top with figs.

nutritional count per serving *30.8g total fat (18g saturated fat); 2370kJ (567 cal); 60.5g carbohydrate; 10.2g protein; 3.7g fibre*

CHOCOLATE & CARAMEL PUDDINGS

1 Preheat oven to 200°C/400°F. Grease four 1-cup (250ml) ovenproof dishes.

2 Beat butter and sugar in a small bowl with an electric mixer until light and fluffy. Beat in eggs, one at a time. Stir in sifted flour, cocoa and milk.

3 Divide two-thirds of the mixture into dishes; place three caramel chocolate squares in centre of each dish. Spoon remaining mixture over chocolate; smooth surface.

4 Bake puddings for 20 minutes or until tops are firm to the touch. Serve immediately.

SERVING SUGGESTION Serve topped with pouring cream or ice-cream and dusted with sifted cocoa powder.

PREP + COOK TIME 30 MINUTES

MAKES 4

125G (4 OUNCES) BUTTER, SOFTENED

⅔ CUP (150G) FIRMLY PACKED BROWN SUGAR

2 EGGS

½ CUP (75G) PLAIN (ALL-PURPOSE) FLOUR

¼ CUP (25G) COCOA POWDER

1½ TABLESPOONS MILK

12 CARAMEL-FILLED CHOCOLATE SQUARES (75G)

nutritional count per pudding *33.4g total fat (20.8g saturated fat); 2449kJ (585 cal); 63.2g carbohydrate; 8.2g protein; 2.4g fibre*

APPLE & FIG TARTS

PREP + COOK TIME 30 MINUTES

SERVES 4

1 LARGE APPLE (200G)

375G (12 OUNCE) BLOCK PUFF PASTRY

6 DRIED FIGS (120G), HALVED HORIZONTALLY

20G (¾ OUNCE) BUTTER, MELTED

¼ CUP (90G) GOLDEN SYRUP

¼ CUP (35G) HAZELNUTS, HALVED

1 TEASPOON CINNAMON SUGAR

1 Preheat oven to 220°C/425°F. Grease a large oven tray.

2 Peel apple, slice thinly crossways; remove and discard seeds.

3 Roll pastry out on a lightly floured sheet of baking paper into a 24cm x 30cm (9½-inch x 12-inch) rectangle. Cut in half lengthways. Arrange apple and figs on pastry. Brush rectangles with butter and half the syrup. Top with hazelnuts and sprinkle with sugar. Slide baking paper with tarts onto oven tray.

4 Bake tarts 20 minutes or until pastry is browned. Drizzle hot tarts with remaining golden syrup.

TIP Cinnamon sugar is available in the spice section of the supermarket.

nutritional count per serving *34.5g total fat (16g saturated fat); 2836kJ (677 cal); 81.6g carbohydrate; 9g protein; 7.6g fibre*

FOR A COMPLETELY SMOOTH LEMON CURD,
STRAIN THE MIXTURE THROUGH A FINE
SIEVE TO REMOVE THE TINY PIECES OF RIND.
LEMON CURD CAN BE MADE AHEAD AND WILL
KEEP FOR SEVERAL WEEKS IN THE FRIDGE.

LEMON CURD TARTS

1 Whisk whole eggs, yolks and sugar in a small heavy-based saucepan until smooth. Add rind, juice and butter, whisking continuously over low heat for 5 minutes or until curd thickens. Do not allow mixture to get too hot or it will curdle.

2 Transfer curd mixture to a stainless steel bowl, then place over a bowl of iced water; stir with a whisk occasionally for 5 minutes to cool to room temperature.

3 Place curd in the freezer for 5 minutes to accelerate chilling, but don't forget it, or it will freeze.

4 Meanwhile, beat cream in a small bowl with an electric mixer until soft peaks form.

5 Spoon rounded tablespoons of curd into tart shells, top with cream; serve immediately. Dust with icing (confectioners') sugar just before serving if you like.

TIPS You will need about 2 lemons for this recipe. You can freeze the unused egg whites and use them later in friands, omelettes or a pavlova.

VARIATIONS You can make this recipe with other citrus fruit; simply replace the lemon rind and juice with the same amount of rind and juice of whatever citrus fruit you like – lime, orange, blood orange, mandarin, grapefruit and tangelo would all work well.

PREP + COOK TIME 30 MINUTES

MAKES 12 (1¼ CUPS LEMON CURD)

2 EGGS

2 EGG YOLKS

⅓ CUP (75G) CASTER SUGAR (SUPERFINE SUGAR)

2 TEASPOONS FINELY GRATED LEMON RIND

⅓ CUP (80ML) LEMON JUICE

75G (2½ OUNCES) UNSALTED COLD BUTTER, CHOPPED FINELY

½ CUP (125ML) THICKENED (HEAVY) CREAM

12 X 6CM (2½-INCH) READY-MADE TART SHELLS (96G)

nutritional count per tart *12.7g total fat (7.5g saturated fat); 709kJ (169 cal); 11.7g carbohydrate; 2.4g protein; 0g fibre*

FOOLS

RHUBARB & GINGER BEER FOOLS

PREP + COOK 15 MINUTES SERVES 4

Combine 500g (1 pound) coarsely chopped, trimmed rhubarb, with 2 teaspoons finely grated ginger, ¼ cup (60ml) ginger beer and 2 tablespoons caster (superfine) sugar in a medium saucepan over high heat. Bring to boil. Reduce heat to medium; simmer, stirring occasionally, 7 minutes or until rhubarb is tender. Transfer to a tray to cool. Meanwhile, beat 300ml thickened (heavy) cream in a small bowl with an electric mixer until firm peaks form. Spoon three-quarters of the rhubarb mixture onto cream; do not stir. Spoon cream mixture into four ⅔ cup (160ml) glasses. Top with remaining rhubarb and ¼ cup (55g) crushed gingernut biscuits.

TIP Rhubarb mixture can be made a day ahead; store refrigerated in an airtight container.

PEACH & VANILLA YOGHURT FOOLS

PREP + COOK TIME 10 MINUTES SERVES 4

Halve 4 medium peaches (600g), discard stones; quarter each half. Process half the peaches with 2 tablespoons caster (superfine) sugar and ¼ teaspoon vanilla extract until smooth. Place 2 cups (560g) vanilla yoghurt in a medium bowl. Spoon three-quarters of the peach puree onto yoghurt; do not stir. Spoon yoghurt mixture into four ⅔ cup (160ml) glasses. Top with remaining puree, remaining peaches, 2 tablespoons coarsely chopped pistachios and 1 tablespoon small mint leaves.

TIP Make double the peach puree and use one quantity to make bellini cocktails: place 1 tablespoon peach puree in each champagne flute and top with sparkling white wine.

CHERRY & LEMONADE FOOLS

PREP + COOK 15 MINUTES SERVES 4

Pit 225g (7 ounces) fresh cherries, reserving 4 cherries on the stem to serve. Place pitted cherries and ⅓ cup (80ml) lemonade in a small frying pan over high heat; bring to the boil. Reduce heat; simmer 5 minutes, mashing with a fork a few times during cooking, or until cherries soften slightly and liquid thickens slightly. Cool. Meanwhile, beat 300ml thickened (heavy) cream in a small bowl with an electric mixer until soft peaks form. Fold ⅓ cup (110g) ready-made lemon curd and ⅓ cup (15g) toasted coconut flakes into cream. Spoon three-quarters of the cherry mixture onto cream mixture; do not stir. Spoon cream mixture into four ⅔ cup (160ml) glasses. Top with remaining cherry mixture, reserved cherries and 1 tablespoon extra toasted coconut.

TIPS Cherry mixture can be made a day ahead; refrigerate in an airtight container. Lemon curd is available from supermarkets.

BLUEBERRY & ORANGE FOOLS

PREP + COOK 10 MINUTES SERVES 4

Combine 125g (4 ounces) blueberries, 1 tablespoon caster (superfine) sugar, 2 teaspoons finely grated orange rind and ¼ cup (60ml) orange juice in a small frying pan over high heat; bring to the boil. Reduce heat; simmer 3 minutes, stirring occasionally or until blueberries soften slightly and liquid thickens slightly. Fold 2 teaspoons finely grated orange rind into 2 cups (550g) thick ready-made custard. Spoon three-quarters blueberry mixture over custard; do not stir. Spoon custard mixture into four ⅔ cup (160ml) glasses. Top with remaining blueberry mixture, 6 sponge finger biscuits (130g) and 60g (2 ounces) blueberries. Serve immediately.

TIPS You will need 1 orange for this recipe. Thick ready-made custard is sold in the refrigerated section of supermarkets.

SMOOTH RICOTTA, SOLD IN TUBS, IS MUCH WETTER
THAN THE FIRM RICOTTA CUT FROM A WHEEL.
IF YOU USE THE FIRM RICOTTA, YOU WILL NEED TO
INCREASE THE AMOUNT OF BUTTERMILK BY ¼ CUP.

BLUEBERRY RICOTTA PIKELETS WITH CARAMELISED ORANGES

PREP + COOK TIME 30 MINUTES

SERVES 6

2 CUPS (300G) SELF-RAISING FLOUR

**¼ CUP (55G) CASTER SUGAR
(SUPERFINE SUGAR)**

2 EGGS

1 CUP (240G) SMOOTH RICOTTA

1¼ CUP (310ML) BUTTERMILK

**2 TEASPOONS FINELY GRATED
ORANGE RIND**

125G (4 OUNCES) FRESH BLUEBERRIES

COOKING-OIL SPRAY

CARAMELISED ORANGES

4 MEDIUM ORANGES (960G)

**¾ CUP (165G) CASTER SUGAR
(SUPERFINE SUGAR)**

¾ CUP (180ML) WATER

¾ CUP (180ML) ORANGE JUICE

1 Process flour, sugar, eggs, ricotta, buttermilk and rind until combined. Transfer batter to a large jug; stir in berries.

2 Spray a heated large heavy-based frying pan with cooking oil. Pour 1 tablespoon batter for each pikelet into pan. Cook pikelets over medium heat until bubbles appear on surface; turn, brown other side. Remove from pan; cover to keep warm. Repeat with remaining batter.

3 Make caramelised oranges.

4 Serve pikelets with caramelised oranges.

CARAMELISED ORANGES Segment oranges over a small bowl. Stir sugar and the water in a medium saucepan over low heat, without boiling, until sugar dissolves. Bring to the boil; boil 10 minutes or until a caramel forms. Remove from heat, carefully stir in juice (take care as caramel will splatter); stir over heat until caramel pieces are dissolved. Stir in orange segments.

TIP To segment oranges, cut off the rind with the white pith, following the curve of the fruit. Cut down either side of each segment close to the membrane to release the segment.

nutritional count per serving *6.7g total fat (3.4g saturated fat); 2050kJ (490 cal); 90.4g carbohydrate; 14.8g protein; 5.5g fibre*

UNLIKE MOST CHOCOLATE MOUSSE RECIPES, THIS ONE CAN BE SERVED THE MINUTE IT IS MADE. IF YOU DO WISH TO MAKE IT A DAY AHEAD, REFRIGERATE, COVERED, THEN BRING TO ROOM TEMPERATURE BEFORE SERVING. YOU COULD ALSO TOP EACH SERVING WITH CHERRIES.

DARK CHOCOLATE & RICOTTA MOUSSE

1 Stir syrup, cocoa, the water and extract in a small saucepan over medium heat; bring to the boil. Remove from heat; cool.

2 Place chocolate in a small heatproof bowl over a small saucepan of simmering water (don't let the water touch the base of the bowl); stir until melted and smooth.

3 Process dates and milk until dates are finely chopped. Add ricotta; process until smooth. Add melted chocolate; process until well combined.

4 Spoon mousse into six ¾ cup (180ml) serving glasses. Spoon cocoa syrup on mousse; top with pomegranate seeds and nuts.

TIP Fresh pomegranate seeds can sometimes be found in the fridge section of supermarkets or good green grocers. If they're not available, cut a whole pomegranate in half crossways; hold it, cut-side down, in the palm of your hand over a bowl, then hit the outside firmly with a wooden spoon. The seeds should fall out easily; discard any white pith that falls out with them. Pomegranate seeds will keep in the fridge for up to a week.

PREP + COOK TIME 20 MINUTES

SERVES 6

⅓ CUP (110G) RICE MALT SYRUP

1 TABLESPOON DUTCH-PROCESSED COCOA

2 TABLESPOONS WATER

½ TEASPOON VANILLA EXTRACT

200G (6½ OUNCES) DARK CHOCOLATE (70% COCOA), CHOPPED

8 FRESH DATES (160G), PITTED

½ CUP (125ML) MILK

2 CUPS (480G) SOFT RICOTTA

2 TABLESPOONS POMEGRANATE SEEDS

2 TABLESPOONS CHOPPED PISTACHIOS

nutritional count per serving *21g total fat (12g saturated fat); 2020kJ (482 cal); 62g carbohydrate; 12.3g protein; 3.8g fibre*

FREEFORM TIRAMISU

PREP TIME 10 MINUTES

SERVES 4

½ CUP (125ML) STRONG ESPRESSO COFFEE, COOLED

½ CUP (125ML) COFFEE-FLAVOURED LIQUEUR

10 SPONGE FINGER BISCUITS (120G), HALVED CROSSWAYS

⅔ CUP (160ML) THICKENED (HEAVY) CREAM

¼ CUP (40G) ICING SUGAR (CONFECTIONERS' SUGAR)

250G (8 OUNCES) MASCARPONE

50G (1½ OUNCES) DARK (SEMI-SWEET) CHOCOLATE

1 Combine coffee and ⅓ cup of the liqueur in a small bowl. Dip biscuits, one at a time, into coffee mixture. Line four 1-cup (250ml) glasses with biscuits; drizzle with any remaining coffee mixture.

2 Beat cream and sifted icing sugar in a small bowl with an electric mixer until soft peaks form; beat in mascarpone and remaining liqueur just until combined. Divide among glasses.

3 Using a vegetable peeler, shave a little chocolate over each tiramisu.

TO MAKE STRONG COFFEE, DISSOLVE 2 TABLESPOONS INSTANT ESPRESSO COFFEE GRANULES IN ½ CUP BOILING WATER. IF YOU HAVE A COFFEE MACHINE, MAKE ENOUGH ESPRESSO SHOTS TO GIVE YOU THE SAME QUANTITY.

nutritional count per serving *54.7g total fat (35.8g saturated fat); 3082kJ (736 cal); 49g carbohydrate; 7g protein; 0.7g fibre*

THERE ARE TWO TYPES OF PERSIMMONS AVAILABLE IN AUTUMN: ASTRINGENT AND NON-ASTRINGENT. THE FIRST, IS HEART SHAPED AND IS EATEN VERY RIPE, OTHERWISE IT WILL TASTE VERY ASTRINGENT. THE OTHER, WHICH IS SOMETIMES SOLD AS FUJI FRUIT (FUJI BEING THE JAPANESE WORD FOR PERSIMMON) IS SQUAT AND EATEN CRISP. YOU CAN USE EITHER VARIETY FOR THIS RECIPE. IF YOU USE THE ASTRINGENT PERSIMMON, IT IS BEST TO SCRAPE AWAY THE FLESH FROM THE SKIN WHEN EATING.

HONEY & LIME BAKED PERSIMMONS

1 Preheat oven to 200°C/400°F. Cut four 35cm (14-inch) pieces of baking paper.

2 Place pieces of paper lengthways in front of you then divide persimmon wedges among baking paper, placing them crossways in the centre. Top with lime slices and ginger; dizzle with honey. Bring short edges of paper together, fold over several times to secure, then tuck sides under to form a parcel. Place parcels on two oven trays.

3 Bake parcels 15 minutes or until persimmon is soft. Serve opened parcels topped with spoonfuls of frozen yoghurt and lime rind.

TIP Use a zester to make the lime rind strips. If you don't have one, you can finely grate the rind instead.

PREP + COOK TIME 25 MINUTES

SERVES 4

4 PERSIMMONS (1KG), EACH CUT INTO 6 WEDGES

1 LIME, SLICED THINLY

20G (¾ OUNCE) FRESH GINGER, SLICED THINLY

1½ TABLESPOONS HONEY

200G (6½ OUNCES) PASSIONFRUIT FROZEN YOGHURT

1 TABLESPOON LIME RIND STRIPS

nutritional count per serving *3g total fat (1.7g saturated fat); 1197kJ (286 cal); 58g carbohydrate; 4g protein; 7.4g fibre*

RASPBERRY NOUGAT FROZEN PARFAIT

**PREP + COOK TIME 25 MINUTES
(+ FREEZING & REFRIGERATION)**

SERVES 8

2 CUPS (400G) RICOTTA

**¾ CUP (165G) CASTER SUGAR
(SUPERFINE SUGAR)**

**¼ CUP (40G) WHOLE ALMONDS,
ROASTED, CHOPPED COARSELY**

**150G (4½ OUNCES) NOUGAT,
CHOPPED COARSELY**

300ML THICKENED (HEAVY) CREAM

1 CUP (135G) FROZEN RASPBERRIES

1 Line base and sides of a 14cm x 21cm (5½-inch x 8½-inch) loaf pan with foil or baking paper, extending the foil 5cm (2-inches) over two long sides.

2 Blend or process ricotta and sugar until smooth; transfer to a large bowl. Stir in nuts and nougat.

3 Beat cream in a small bowl with an electric mixer until soft peaks form. Fold cream into ricotta mixture; fold in raspberries.

4 Spoon mixture into pan, cover with foil; freeze until firm.

5 Before serving, place parfait in the fridge for 15 minutes to soften slightly. Turn parfait out onto a board and cut into slices.

TIPS Before you cut the parfait into slices, dip the knife in hot water first; this will make it easier to cut. The parfait can be made and frozen up to 1 week ahead.

SERVING SUGGESTION Serve with a raspberry compote: cook 2½ cups (330g) frozen raspberries with ¼ cup (55g) caster (superfine) sugar in a medium saucepan, stirring, over low heat, until berries are very soft. Push mixture through a coarse sieve into a medium bowl; discard seeds. Just before serving, stir 500g (1 pound) fresh raspberries into sauce.

nutritional count per serving *23.5g total fat (11.9g saturated fat); 1648kJ (394 cal); 38.6g carbohydrate; 7.7g protein; 1.4g fibre*

STONE FRUIT WITH BERRY ROSEWATER YOGHURT

1 Make berry rosewater yoghurt.

2 Divide peach, nectarine, plum and apricot between two bowls.

3 Spoon yoghurt over fruit; sprinkle with nuts.

BERRY ROSEWATER YOGHURT Blend or process strawberries with rosewater until smooth. Swirl through yoghurt.

YOU CAN USE THAWED FROZEN STRAWBERRIES OR RASPBERRIES FOR THIS RECIPE. AND EITHER WHITE OR YELLOW PEACHES AND NECTARINES.

PREP + COOK TIME 10 MINUTES

SERVES 2

1 MEDIUM WHITE PEACH (150G), SLICED THINLY

1 MEDIUM YELLOW NECTARINE (170G), SLICED THINLY

1 PLUM (110G), SLICED THINLY

1 APRICOT (75G), SLICED THINLY

2 TABLESPOONS COARSELY CHOPPED PISTACHIOS

BERRY ROSEWATER YOGHURT

150G (4½ OUNCES) STRAWBERRIES, SLICED

1 TABLESPOON ROSEWATER

1 CUP (280G) LOW-FAT VANILLA YOGHURT

nutritional count per serving *6.8g total fat (1.1g saturated fat); 1223kJ (292 cal); 38.7g carbohydrate; 13.4g protein; 6.7g fibre*

CHOC-CHERRY & HAZELNUT BISCOTTI TRIFLE

PREP TIME 15 MINUTES

SERVES 4

300G (9½ OUNCES) FROZEN PITTED BLACK CHERRIES, THAWED

⅓ CUP (80ML) MARSALA

170G (5½ OUNCES) CHOCOLATE HAZELNUT BISCOTTI

375G (12 OUNCES) CHOCOLATE MOUSSE

1 Combine cherries and marsala in a small bowl.

2 Reserve eight biscotti; coarsely chop remaining biscotti.

3 Whisk chocolate mousse in a medium bowl until smooth.

4 Spoon half the cherry mixture into four 2-cup (500ml) glasses; top with half the chopped biscotti and half the mousse. Repeat layering.

5 Serve trifles with reserved biscotti.

YOU CAN IMPROVISE WITH THE INGREDIENTS IN THIS TRIFLE. TRY SPONGE FINGER BISCUITS INSTEAD OF BISCOTTI, RASPBERRIES IN PLACE OF CHERRIES AND A NUT-FLAVOURED LIQUEUR AS A SUBSTITUTE FOR THE MARSALA.

nutritional count per serving *18.8g total fat (10.4g saturated fat); 1935kJ (463 cal); 56.4g carbohydrate; 10.1g protein; 2.4g fibre*

BERRY HAZELNUT CUPS

1 Blend or process half the raspberries and half the icing sugar until smooth; strain through a fine sieve into a small jug.

2 Beat cream, liqueur and remaining icing sugar in a small bowl with an electric mixer until soft peaks form.

3 Spoon cream into brandy baskets; top with remaining raspberries and the nuts. Drizzle with raspberry sauce.

PREP TIME 25 MINUTES

SERVES 6

250G (8 OUNCES) RASPBERRIES

2 TABLESPOONS ICING SUGAR (CONFECTIONERS SUGAR')

300ML THICKENED (HEAVY) CREAM

2 TABLESPOONS HAZELNUT-FLAVOURED LIQUEUR

6 BRANDY BASKETS (90G)

⅓ CUP (45G) COARSELY CHOPPED ROASTED PEELED HAZELNUTS

nutritional count per serving *40.4g total fat (23.5g saturated fat); 2174kJ (520 cal); 26.9g carbohydrate; 4.7g protein; 5.4g fibre*

137

SALT & FIVE-SPICE CHICKEN (PAGE 19)

ASIAN BANQUET FOR FOUR

If you prefer, you can serve the chicken first with ice-cold beers, then proceed to the salad and larb. With the larb, omit the rice noodles from the recipe and instead serve it with the separated leaves of 1 butter (boston) lettuce for people to fill with larb and wrap themselves.

BANQUET

SALT & FIVE-SPICE CHICKEN (PAGE 19)

BARBECUED CHILLI PRAWNS WITH GREEN MANGO SALAD (PAGE 33)

PORK LARB WITH RICE NOODLES (PAGE 16)

DESSERT

HONEY & LIME BAKED PERSIMMONS (PAGE 129)

LIGHT & HEALTHY FOR TWO

Both the soup and dessert recipes are the perfect quantity for two people. For the salad, instead buy a 400g (12½-ounce) piece of rump steak (cook it for the same time) and 175g (5½ ounces) spinach. Keep the other quantities the same and drizzle with the amount of dressing to taste.

STARTER

CHICKEN & CORN SOUP (PAGE 15)

MAIN

BEEF & MIXED SPROUT SALAD (PAGE 20)

DESSERT

STONE FRUIT WITH BERRY ROSEWATER YOGHURT (PAGE 133)

BEEF & MIXED SPROUT SALAD (PAGE 20)

RICOTTA & SPINACH AGNOLOTTI (PAGE 69)

SMART ITALIAN LUNCH FOR SIX

You will need to double the salad recipe here; serve it at the same time as the pizza, allowing your guests to help themselves. You could also combine an assortment of olives and serve these alongside as well.

STARTERS

ROAST BEEF & PANZANELLA SALAD (PAGE 8)

TALEGGIO, PROSCIUTTO & ROCKET PIZZA (PAGE 96)

MAIN

RICOTTA & SPINACH AGNOLOTTI (PAGE 69)

DESSERT

RASPBERRY NOUGAT FROZEN PARFAIT (PAGE 130)

BRUNCH FEAST FOR SIX

The fun part of a feast is the sense of plenty provided by displaying all the dishes for each course at once. Not only is it easier on the host it also means that your guests will interact with each other more.

SAVOURY

CARAMELISED ONION & GOAT'S CHEESE QUICHES (PAGE 86)

SMOKED SALMON & ROCKET BRUSCHETTA (PAGE 42)

MOROCCAN LAMB CUTLETS WITH COUSCOUS SALAD (PAGE 81)

SWEET

BLUEBERRY RICOTTA PIKELETS WITH CARAMELISED ORANGES (PAGE 122)

BERRY HAZELNUT CUPS (PAGE 137)

BLUEBERRY RICOTTA PIKELETS WITH CARAMELISED ORANGES (PAGE 122)

139

GLOSSARY

ALMONDS
blanched brown skins removed.
flaked paper-thin slices.
ground also called almond meal; nuts are powdered to a coarse flour-like texture.

BREADCRUMBS, PANKO (JAPANESE) have a lighter texture than Western-style breadcrumbs. They are available from most supermarkets and Asian food stores.

BROCCOLINI a cross between broccoli and chinese kale; long asparagus-like stems with a long loose floret, both completely edible. While it resembles broccoli it is milder and sweeter in taste.

BUTTER we use salted butter unless stated otherwise; 125g is equal to 1 stick (4 ounces).

CAPSICUM (BELL PEPPER) available in many colours: red, green, yellow, orange and purplish-black. Be sure to discard seeds and membranes before use.

CHEESE
blue mould-treated cheeses mottled with blue veining. Varieties include firm and crumbly stilton types and mild, creamy brie-like cheeses.
fetta Greek in origin; a crumbly textured goat- or sheep-milk cheese having a sharp, salty taste. Ripened and stored in salted whey; particularly good cubed and tossed into salads.
goat's made from goat's milk, has an earthy, strong taste. Available in soft, crumbly and firm textures, in various shapes and sizes, and sometimes rolled in ash or herbs.
haloumi a Greek Cypriot cheese with a semi-firm, spongy texture and very salty sweet flavour. Ripened and stored in salted whey; best grilled or fried, it holds its shape well on being heated. Eat while still warm as it becomes tough and rubbery on cooling.
mozzarella soft, spun-curd cheese; originating in southern Italy where it was traditionally made from water-buffalo milk. Now made from cow's milk, it is the most popular pizza cheese because of its low melting point and elasticity when heated.

ricotta a soft, sweet, moist, white cow's-milk cheese with a low fat content and a slightly grainy texture.

CHICKEN
breast fillets breast halved, skinned and boned.
thigh fillets the skin and bone removed.

CHILLI use rubber gloves when seeding and chopping fresh chillies as they can burn your skin. Removing membranes and seeds lessens the heat level.
green any unripened chilli; also some particular varieties that are ripe when green, such as jalapeño, habanero, poblano or serrano.
long red available both fresh and dried; a generic term used for any moderately hot, thin, long (6-8cm/2¼-3¼-inch) chilli.

CHINESE COOKING WINE (SHAO HSING) also called chinese rice wine; made from fermented rice, wheat, sugar and salt. Found in Asian food shops; if you can't find it, use mirin or sherry.

CHINESE FIVE-SPICE also known as five-spice powder; a fragrant mixture of ground cinnamon, cloves, star anise, sichuan pepper and fennel seeds.

CHOCOLATE, DARK (SEMI-SWEET) also called luxury chocolate; made of a high percentage of cocoa liquor and cocoa butter, and little added sugar.

CIABATTA BREAD in Italian, the word means slipper, the traditional shape of this popular crisp-crusted, open-textured white sourdough bread.

COCOA POWDER also called cocoa; dried, unsweetened, roasted and ground cocoa beans (cacao seeds).
dutch-processed is treated with an alkali to neutralise its acids. It has a reddish-brown colour, a mild flavour and is easy to dissolve.

COCONUT
flaked dried flaked coconut flesh.
milk not the liquid found inside the fruit (coconut water), but the diluted liquid from the second pressing of the white flesh of a mature coconut. Available in cans and cartons at most supermarkets.

COUSCOUS a fine, dehydrated, grain-like cereal product made from semolina; it swells to three or four times its original size when liquid is added.

CREAM
pouring also known as pure or fresh cream. It has no additives and contains a minimum fat content of 35%.
thickened (heavy) a whipping cream that contains a thickener. It has a minimum fat content of 35%.

FISH SAUCE called naam pla (Thai) and nuoc naam (Vietnamese); the two are almost identical. Made from pulverised salted fermented fish (usually anchovies); has a pungent smell and strong taste. Available in varying degrees of intensity, use according to your taste.

FLOUR
plain (all-purpose) unbleached wheat flour; is the best for baking.
rice very fine, almost powdery, gluten-free flour; made from ground white rice. Used in baking, as a thickener, and in some Asian noodles and desserts.
self-raising plain or wholemeal flour with baking powder and salt added.

GINGER, FRESH also called green or root ginger; the thick gnarled root of a tropical plant.

GREASING/OILING PANS use butter or margarine (for sweet baking), oil or cooking-oil spray (for savoury baking) to grease pans; overgreasing can cause food to overbrown.

HORSERADISH CREAM a commercial paste of grated horseradish, mustard seeds, oil and sugar. Available in bottles from most supermarkets.

KAFFIR LIME LEAVES also called bai magrood, sold fresh, dried or frozen; looks like two glossy dark green leaves joined end to end, forming a rounded hourglass shape. A strip of fresh lime peel may be substituted for each kaffir lime leaf.

KUMARA (ORANGE SWEET POTATO)
Polynesian name of an orange-fleshed sweet potato often confused with yam.

LAMB
backstrap also called eye of loin; the larger fillet from a row of loin chops or cutlets. A tender cut, so is best cooked rapidly: barbecued or pan-fried.
cutlet small, tender rib chop; sometimes sold french-trimmed, with all the fat and gristle at the end of the bone removed.

LEMON GRASS a tall, clumping, lemon-smelling and tasting, sharp-edged aromatic tropical grass; the white lower part of the stem is used, finely chopped, in many South-East Asian dishes. Can be found fresh, dried, powdered and frozen, in supermarkets, greengrocers and Asian food shops.

MIRIN a Japanese champagne-coloured cooking wine, made of glutinous rice and alcohol. It is used just for cooking and should not be confused with sake.

MIXED SPICE a classic ground spice mixture generally containing caraway, allspice, coriander, cumin, nutmeg and ginger, although cinnamon and other spices can be added.

NOODLES
bean thread also called cellophane or glass noodles, these are made from a paste of water and mung bean flour. To soften, it is best to soak them in hot water as they lose texture when boiled.
rice stick popular South-East Asian dried rice noodle, also called kway teow. They come in different widths (thin used in soups, wide in stir-fries), but all should be soaked in hot water to soften.

OIL
cooking spray we use a cholesterol-free cooking spray made from canola oil.
olive made from ripened olives. Extra virgin and virgin are the first and second press, respectively, of the olives and are therefore considered the best; "light" refers to taste not fat levels.
peanut pressed from ground peanuts; the most commonly used oil in Asian cooking because of its capacity to handle high heat without burning.
sesame roasted, crushed, white sesame seeds; used as a flavouring rather than a cooking medium.

ONION
green (scallions) also called, incorrectly, shallot; an immature onion picked before the bulb has formed, has a long, bright-green stalk.
red also called spanish or bermuda onion; a sweet-flavoured, large, purple-red onion.

PERSIMMONS there are two types available: astringent and non-astringent. Astringent persimmons are heart shaped and eaten very ripe, otherwise the taste is very astringent. Non-astringent persimmons, sometimes sold as fuji fruit (Japanese for persimmon), are squat shaped and eaten crisp.

PINE NUTS also called pignoli; not a nut but a small, cream-coloured kernel from pine cones. They are best toasted before use to bring out the flavour.

POMEGRANATE dark-red, leathery-skinned fresh fruit about the size of an orange filled with hundreds of seeds, each wrapped in an edible lucent-crimson pulp having a unique tangy sweet-sour flavour.

PRESERVED LEMON RIND a North African specialty; lemons are quartered and preserved in salt and lemon juice or water. To use, remove and discard pulp. Squeeze juice from rind, then rinse well and slice thinly. Sold in delicatessens and major supermarkets.

QUINCE PASTE a thick quince preserve which can be sliced; usually served on a cheese platter. Available from most supermarkets and delicatessens.

RAS EL HANOUT a classic Moroccan spice blend; meaning 'top of the shop', it is the very best blend a spice merchant has to offer. Most versions contain over a dozen spices including cardamom, mace, nutmeg, cinnamon and ground chilli.

RHUBARB a plant with long, green-red stalks; rhubarb becomes sweet and edible when cooked.

ROCKET (ARUGULA) also called rugula and rucola; peppery green leaf eaten raw in salads or used in cooking. Baby rocket leaves are smaller and less peppery.

ROSEWATER extract made from crushed rose petals; used for its aromatic quality in sweetmeats and desserts.

SAMBAL OELEK also called ulek or olek; an Indonesian salty paste made from ground chillies and vinegar.

SPINACH also called english spinach. Baby spinach leaves are best eaten raw in salads; the larger leaves are cooked until barely wilted.

SUGAR
brown a very soft, finely granulated sugar that retains molasses for its colour and flavour.
caster (superfine) finely granulated table sugar.
icing (confectioners') also known as powdered sugar; pulverised granulated sugar crushed together with a small amount of cornflour (cornstarch).
palm also called nam tan pip, jaggery, jawa or gula melaka; made from the sap of the sugar palm tree. Light brown to black in colour and usually sold in rock-hard cakes; use brown sugar if it's not available.

VINEGAR, MALT vinegar made from fermented malt and beech shavings.

WATERCRESS one of the cress family, a large group of peppery greens used raw in salads, dips and sandwiches, or cooked in soups. Highly perishable, it must be used as soon as possible after purchase.

YOGHURT we use plain full-cream yoghurt in our recipes.
Greek-style plain yoghurt strained in a cloth (traditionally muslin) to remove the whey and to give it a creamy consistency.

CONVERSION CHART

MEASURES

One Australian metric measuring cup holds approximately 250ml; one Australian metric tablespoon holds 20ml; one Australian metric teaspoon holds 5ml.

The difference between one country's measuring cups and another's is within a two- or three-teaspoon variance, and will not affect your cooking results. North America, New Zealand and the United Kingdom use a 15ml tablespoon.

All cup and spoon measurements are level. The most accurate way of measuring dry ingredients is to weigh them. When measuring liquids, use a clear glass or plastic jug with the metric markings.

The imperial measurements used in these recipes are approximate only. Measurements for cake pans are approximate only. Using same-shaped cake pans of a similar size should not affect the outcome of your baking. We measure the inside top of the cake pan to determine sizes.

We use large eggs with an average weight of 60g (2 ounces).

DRY MEASURES

METRIC	IMPERIAL
15g	½oz
30g	1oz
60g	2oz
90g	3oz
125g	4oz (¼lb)
155g	5oz
185g	6oz
220g	7oz
250g	8oz (½lb)
280g	9oz
315g	10oz
345g	11oz
375g	12oz (¾lb)
410g	13oz
440g	14oz
470g	15oz
500g	16oz (1lb)
750g	24oz (1½lb)
1kg	32oz (2lb)

LIQUID MEASURES

METRIC	IMPERIAL
30ml	1 fluid oz
60ml	2 fluid oz
100ml	3 fluid oz
125ml	4 fluid oz
150ml	5 fluid oz
190ml	6 fluid oz
250ml	8 fluid oz
300ml	10 fluid oz
500ml	16 fluid oz
600ml	20 fluid oz
1000ml (1 litre)	1¾ pints

LENGTH MEASURES

METRIC	IMPERIAL
3mm	⅛in
6mm	¼in
1cm	½in
2cm	¾in
2.5cm	1in
5cm	2in
6cm	2½in
8cm	3in
10cm	4in
13cm	5in
15cm	6in
18cm	7in
20cm	8in
22cm	9in
25cm	10in
28cm	11in
30cm	12in (1ft)

OVEN TEMPERATURES

The oven temperatures in this book are for conventional ovens; if you have a fan-forced oven, decrease the temperature by 10-20 degrees.

	°C (CELSIUS)	°F (FAHRENHEIT)
Very slow	120	250
Slow	150	300
Moderately slow	160	325
Moderate	180	350
Moderately hot	200	400
Hot	220	425
Very hot	240	475

INDEX

slow
fast

THE AUSTRALIAN
Women's Weekly

slow
fast

CONTENTS

SLOW LUNCHES

LABNE ARE BALLS OF FRESH CHEESE MADE FROM DRAINED YOGHURT, AND THEN MARINATED IN OLIVE OIL. LABNE IS AVAILABLE FROM DELICATESSENS AND SOME SUPERMARKETS. YOU CAN USE CRUMBLED FETTA OR SOFT GOAT'S CHEESE INSTEAD.

WARM CHICKEN, LABNE & MAPLE WALNUT SALAD

PREP + COOK TIME 1 HOUR

SERVES 6

500G (1 POUND) BABY BEETROOT (BEETS)

¼ CUP (60ML) OLIVE OIL

300G (9½ OUNCES) UNPEELED PUMPKIN, CUT INTO THIN WEDGES

¾ CUP (75G) WALNUT HALVES

2 TABLESPOONS MAPLE SYRUP

600G (1¼ POUNDS) CHICKEN BREAST FILLETS

1½ TABLESPOONS SHERRY OR RED WINE VINEGAR

2 TEASPOONS WHOLEGRAIN MUSTARD

1 TEASPOON DIJON MUSTARD

125G (4 OUNCES) MIXED SALAD LEAVES

100G (3 OUNCES) DRAINED LABNE

1 Preheat oven to 200°C/400°F.

2 Trim beetroot, leaving 2.5cm (1-inch) of stems attached. Cut beetroot in half. Place beetroot in a roasting pan; drizzle with 1 tablespoon of the oil. Bake 15 minutes.

3 Add pumpkin to beetroot; bake further 25 minutes or until vegetables are tender.

4 Meanwhile, place nuts on a baking-paper-lined oven tray; drizzle with syrup. Bake 10 minutes or until browned, stirring halfway through. Cool.

5 Preheat barbecue (or chargrill plate or grill) to high heat. Brush chicken with 2 teaspoons of the oil; season. Cook chicken 3 minutes each side or until cooked through. Remove from heat, cover; rest 5 minutes.

6 Meanwhile, combine vinegar, mustards and remaining oil in a small bowl. Season to taste.

7 Slice chicken thickly. Arrange salad leaves on a platter; top with pumpkin, beetroot, chicken, nuts and labne. Drizzle with dressing.

nutritional count per serving *23.1g total fat (4.7g saturated fat); 1619kJ (387 cal); 16.7g carbohydrate; 28.4g protein; 4.3g fibre*

ASIAN-STYLE FISH CAKES

1 Preheat grill (broiler) to high. Place fish on an oiled foil-lined tray; season with salt and pepper. Cook under grill for 12 minutes or until fish is just cooked through. Cool.

2 Boil, steam or microwave potatoes until tender; drain. Mash potatoes in a large bowl until smooth.

3 Flake cooled fish into mashed potato, continue mashing with fork until fish flakes are broken into smaller pieces.

4 Add green onion, garlic, ginger, chilli and egg to potato mixture; stir well to combine ingredients (mixture will be quite moist). Season. Divide mixture into 12 portions. Using damp hands, shape mixture into 7cm (2¾-inch) patties. Refrigerate 10 minutes.

5 Meanwhile, make dressing.

6 Place breadcrumbs in a shallow bowl; gently coat patties in crumbs.

7 Heat oil in a large heavy-based frying pan over medium heat. Cook fish cakes, in two batches, for 4 minutes each side or until heated through and golden on both sides.

8 Serve fish cakes with dressing.

DRESSING Combine ingredients in a small bowl.

SERVING SUGGESTION Serve with baby Asian salad leaves.

PREP + COOK TIME 45 MINUTES (+ COOLING & REFRIGERATION)

SERVES 4

800G (1½ POUNDS) FIRM WHITE FISH FILLETS

3 MEDIUM POTATOES (600G), CHOPPED COARSELY

2 GREEN ONIONS (SCALLIONS), SLICED FINELY

1 CLOVE GARLIC, CRUSHED

1 TABLESPOON FINELY GRATED FRESH GINGER

1 FRESH SMALL RED CHILLI, CHOPPED FINELY

1 EGG, BEATEN LIGHTLY

1½ CUPS (110G) PANKO (JAPANESE) BREADCRUMBS

½ CUP (125ML) OLIVE OIL

DRESSING

2 TABLESPOONS MIRIN

⅓ CUP (80ML) SOY SAUCE

2 TABLESPOONS FISH SAUCE

2 FRESH SMALL RED CHILLIES, SEEDED CHOPPED FINELY

⅓ CUP (80ML) LIME JUICE

2 GREEN ONIONS (SCALLIONS), SLICED FINELY

nutritional count per serving *33.8g total fat (6g saturated fat); 2826kJ (675 cal); 40.4g carbohydrate; 49.2g protein; 4.6g fibre*

11

ROAST SALMON WITH FENNEL & APPLE SALAD

PREP + COOK TIME 1 HOUR 15 MINUTES (+ STANDING)

SERVES 10

½ CUP (80G) CURRANTS

1½ CUPS (375ML) VERJUICE

2.5KG (5-POUND) WHOLE SALMON, CLEANED

1 MEDIUM BROWN ONION (150G), SLICED THINLY

1 MEDIUM LEMON (140G), SLICED

4 FRESH BAY LEAVES

6 STEMS FRESH BASIL

40G (1½ OUNCES) BUTTER

80G (2½ OUNCES) FRESH FLAT-LEAF PARSLEY, STEMS ATTACHED

1 LARGE FENNEL BULB (550G)

2 SMALL GREEN-SKINNED APPLES (160G)

¼ CUP (60ML) EXTRA VIRGIN OLIVE OIL

1 Combine currants and ½ cup of the verjuice in a small bowl. Cover; stand until required.

2 Preheat oven to 200°C/400°F.

3 Wipe salmon cavity clean; season inside and out. Fill cavity with onion, lemon, bay leaves and basil. Secure opening with skewers.

4 Line a large oven tray with foil, then baking paper; grease paper with butter. Place salmon in the centre. Pour remaining verjuice over salmon; fold foil and paper over salmon to enclose tightly.

5 Bake salmon for 50 minutes or until salmon is almost cooked through. Remove from oven; rest 20 minutes.

6 Meanwhile, pick leaves from parsley; finely chop half the parsley stems. Reserve feathery fronds from fennel. Thinly slice fennel using a mandoline or V-slicer. Peel and core apples; cut into matchsticks using a mandoline or V-slicer.

7 Carefully peel away skin from salmon. Transfer salmon to a large platter.

8 Strain cooking juices into a small saucepan; place over high heat until hot.

9 Place currant mixture, parsley leaves, chopped parsley stems, apple, fennel and oil in a large bowl; toss gently to combine. Season to taste. Top salmon with half the salad.

10 Serve salmon with remaining salad and fennel fronds; drizzle with warm cooking juices.

nutritional count per serving *28.3g total fat (7.7g saturated fat); 1965kJ (469 cal); 13.6g carbohydrate; 43.5g protein; 2.3g fibre*

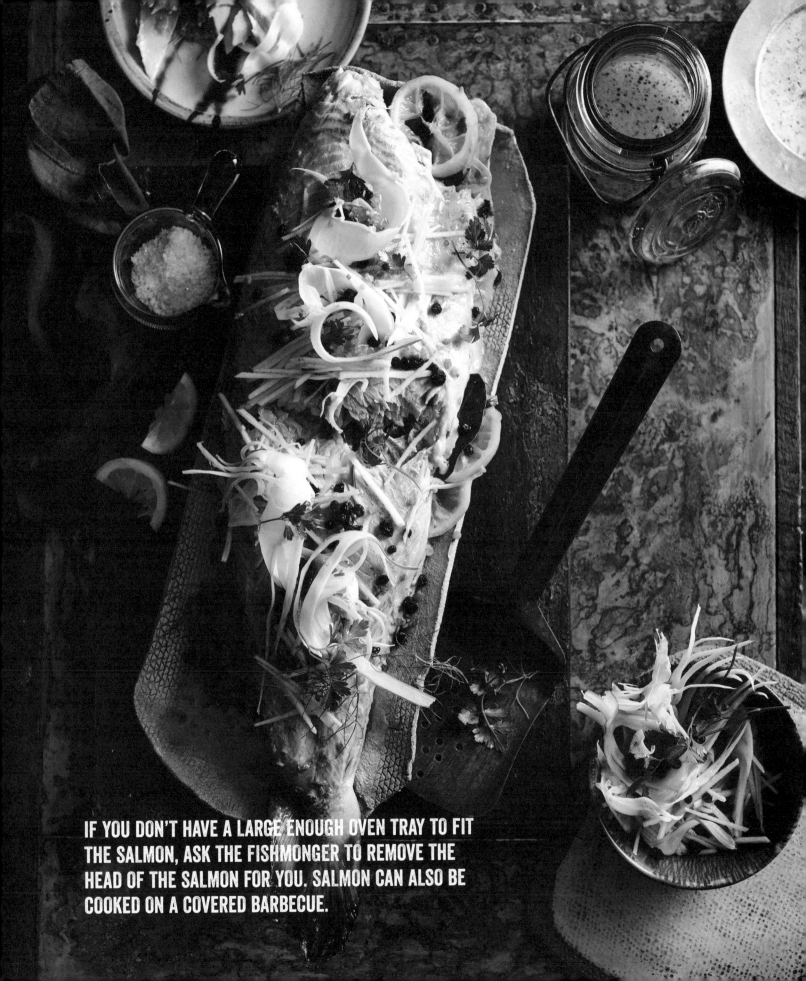

IF YOU DON'T HAVE A LARGE ENOUGH OVEN TRAY TO FIT
THE SALMON, ASK THE FISHMONGER TO REMOVE THE
HEAD OF THE SALMON FOR YOU. SALMON CAN ALSO BE
COOKED ON A COVERED BARBECUE.

SPICY FISH TAGINE WITH RED COUSCOUS

1 Combine rind, chilli, garlic and oil in a large bowl with fish. Cover; refrigerate 3 hours or overnight.

2 Melt butter in a tagine or large frying pan; cook fennel, stirring, until browned lightly. Add beans, raisins, wine and saffron; top with fish. Bring to the boil. Reduce heat to medium-low; simmer, covered, 15 minutes or until fish is just cooked through. Season to taste.

3 Meanwhile, make red couscous.

4 Scatter nuts and reserved fennel fronds over tagine, then serve with red couscous.

RED COUSCOUS Heat oil in a medium saucepan over medium heat; cook harissa, paprika and half the green onion, stirring, for 2 minutes or until fragrant. Add stock and the water; bring to the boil. Remove from heat, add couscous; cover, stand 5 minutes or until liquid is absorbed. Using a fork, fluff couscous then stir in juice; season to taste. Top with remaining green onion.

THIS RECIPE IS FOR LOVERS OF SPICY FOOD. IF YOU PREFER A MILDER FLAVOUR, USE HALF THE AMOUNT OF CHILLI FLAKES AND HARISSA. YOU CAN USE BLUE-EYE TREVALLA, SNAPPER OR ANY OTHER MEATY FIRM WHITE FISH FILLETS IN THIS RECIPE. FISH OR CHICKEN STOCK CAN BE USED INSTEAD OF WINE.

PREP + COOK TIME 40 MINUTES (+ REFRIGERATION)

SERVES 4

1 TABLESPOON FINELY GRATED LEMON RIND

2 TEASPOONS DRIED CHILLI FLAKES

2 CLOVES GARLIC, CRUSHED

1 TABLESPOON OLIVE OIL

4 X 200G (6½-OUNCE) WHITE FISH FILLETS, SKIN ON

30G (1 OUNCE) BUTTER

2 BABY FENNEL BULBS (260G), TRIMMED, CUT INTO WEDGES, FRONDS RESERVED

150G (5 OUNCES) GREEN BEANS, HALVED LENGTHWAYS

⅓ CUP (50G) RAISINS

1 CUP (250ML) DRY WHITE WINE

PINCH SAFFRON THREADS

⅓ CUP (45G) ROASTED PISTACHIOS

RED COUSCOUS

1 TABLESPOON OLIVE OIL

1 TABLESPOON HARISSA PASTE

2 TEASPOONS SWEET PAPRIKA

4 GREEN ONIONS (SCALLIONS), SLICED THINLY

1 CUP (250ML) CHICKEN STOCK

½ CUP (125ML) WATER

1½ CUPS (300G) COUSCOUS

1 TABLESPOON LEMON JUICE

nutritional count per serving *25.3g total fat (7g saturated fat); 3224kJ (770 cal); 71.5g carbohydrate; 53g protein; 8.2g fibre*

BARBECUED BEEF RUMP WITH PANZANELLA SALAD

PREP + COOK TIME 2 HOURS (+ STANDING)

SERVES 8

2 CLOVES GARLIC, CHOPPED

1 TABLESPOON FRESH THYME LEAVES

2 TABLESPOONS OLIVE OIL

2 TABLESPOONS BALSAMIC VINEGAR

3KG (6-POUND) WHOLE RUMP OF BEEF

ANCHOVY BUTTER

8 ANCHOVY FILLETS, CHOPPED

2 CLOVES GARLIC, CHOPPED

2 TABLESPOONS CHOPPED FRESH FLAT-LEAF PARSLEY

1 TABLESPOON CHOPPED FRESH THYME LEAVES

250G (8 OUNCES) BUTTER, SOFTENED, CHOPPED

PANZANELLA SALAD

3 MEDIUM RED CAPSICUMS (BELL PEPPERS) (600G)

3 MEDIUM YELLOW CAPSICUMS (BELL PEPPERS) (600G)

10 MEDIUM RIPE TOMATOES (1.5KG)

⅔ CUP (160ML) EXTRA VIRGIN OLIVE OIL

¼ CUP (60ML) RED WINE VINEGAR

1 LOAF CIABATTA BREAD (440G), CRUSTS REMOVED, CUT INTO 2CM (¾-INCH) PIECES

2 TABLESPOONS BABY CAPERS

2 SHALLOTS (50G), SLICED THINLY

1 CUP TORN FRESH BASIL LEAVES

125G (4 OUNCES) SMALL BLACK OLIVES

1 Combine garlic, thyme, oil and vinegar in a small bowl; rub all over beef. Stand at room temperature 1 hour. Season with freshly ground black pepper and salt.

2 Meanwhile, preheat a covered barbecue to medium.

3 Cook beef on barbecue with the hood down, 1½ hours for medium-rare, or until cooked as desired. Remove from heat, cover loosely with foil; rest for at least 15 minutes (or up to 30 minutes).

4 Meanwhile, make anchovy butter then panzanella salad.

5 Cut beef into thick slices, top with anchovy butter; serve with panzanella salad.

ANCHOVY BUTTER Process ingredients until smooth. Transfer to a small bowl, cover; refrigerate until required.

PANZANELLA SALAD Preheat grill (broiler). Quarter capsicums; discard seeds and membrane. Place, skin-side up, on a large foil-lined oven tray. Place under hot grill for 10 minutes or until skin blisters and blackens. Cover with foil; stand 10 minutes. When capsicum are cool enough to handle, peel away skins. Cut a small cross in the base of each tomato; plunge into boiling water, in batches, for 1 minute or until skin loosens then immediately transfer to a bowl of iced water. Cool. Peel tomatoes; cut into wedges, discard seeds. Whisk oil and vinegar in a small bowl; season to taste. Ten minutes before serving, place capsicum, tomato and dressing in a large bowl with remaining ingredients; toss gently to combine.

YOU CAN ROAST THE BEEF IN A 200°C/400°F OVEN; THE COOKING TIME WILL BE THE SAME. IT IS BEST TO USE DAY-OLD BREAD IN THE PANZANELLA, OR YOU CAN TOAST THE BREAD CUBES FIRST TO DRY THEM OUT A LITTLE.

nutritional count per serving *92.5g total fat (34.7g saturated fat); 6008kJ (1435 cal); 26.3g carbohydrate; 121g protein; 6.7g fibre*

WARM BEEF & HUMMUS SALAD

1 Process chickpeas, tahini, juice, spices, the water and half the oil until smooth. Season to taste.

2 Heat half the remaining oil in a large frying pan over medium heat; cook onion and garlic, stirring, until softened. Add beef, spices and half the chilli; cook, stirring, 15 minutes or until beef is cooked and golden. Add honey; cook 2 minutes or until beef is crisp. Season to taste.

3 Spread hummus on a large platter. Spoon beef mixture onto hummus; top with remaining chilli, remaining oil and the herbs.

SERVING SUGGESTION Serve with char-grilled flat bread.

PREP + COOK TIME 40 MINUTES

SERVES 6

800G (1½ POUNDS) CANNED CHICKPEAS (GARBANZO BEANS), DRAINED, RINSED

⅓ CUP (90G) TAHINI

⅓ CUP (80ML) LEMON JUICE

1 TEASPOON GROUND CORIANDER

1 TEASPOON GROUND CUMIN

¼ CUP (60ML) WATER

⅓ CUP (80ML) OLIVE OIL

1 MEDIUM BROWN ONION (150G), CHOPPED FINELY

3 CLOVES GARLIC, CHOPPED FINELY

500G (1 POUND) MINCED (GROUND) BEEF

1 TEASPOON GROUND ALLSPICE

½ TEASPOON GROUND CINNAMON

1 FRESH LONG RED CHILLI, SLICED THINLY

1 TABLESPOON HONEY

2 TABLESPOONS FRESH FLAT-LEAF PARSLEY LEAVES

2 TABLESPOONS FRESH MINT LEAVES

nutritional count per serving *30.4g total fat (6.4g saturated fat); 1943kJ (464 cal); 18.3g carbohydrate; 26.7g protein; 7.2g fibre*

CHICKEN, BURGHUL & POMEGRANATE SALAD

PREP + COOK TIME 45 MINUTES (+ REFRIGERATION)

SERVES 6

¼ CUP (60ML) OLIVE OIL

¼ CUP (60ML) POMEGRANATE MOLASSES

1 TABLESPOON GROUND CUMIN

2 CLOVES GARLIC, CRUSHED

1KG (2 POUNDS) CHICKEN BREAST FILLETS

1½ CUPS (375ML) CHICKEN STOCK

1½ CUPS (240G) BURGHUL

1 LARGE POMEGRANATE (430G), SEEDS REMOVED

1 MEDIUM RED ONION (170G), HALVED, SLICED THINLY

350G (11 OUNCES) WATERCRESS, TRIMMED

2 CUPS FIRMLY PACKED FRESH FLAT-LEAF PARSLEY LEAVES

1 CUP (110G) COARSELY CHOPPED ROASTED WALNUTS

150G (4½ OUNCES) FETTA, CRUMBLED

POMEGRANATE DRESSING

¼ CUP (60ML) OLIVE OIL

¼ CUP (60ML) LEMON JUICE

3 TEASPOONS HONEY

3 TEASPOONS POMEGRANATE MOLASSES

1 Combine oil, molasses, cumin and garlic in a large bowl with chicken. Cover; refrigerate 3 hours or overnight.

2 Bring stock to the boil in a medium saucepan. Remove from heat, add burghul; cover, stand 5 minutes.

3 Meanwhile, make pomegranate dressing.

4 Drain chicken, discard marinade. Cook chicken on a heated oiled chargrill plate (or barbecue or grill), for 3 minutes each side or until cooked through. Remove chicken from heat, cover loosely with foil; rest 10 minutes, then slice thickly.

5 Place chicken and burghul in a large bowl with dressing and remaining ingredients; toss gently to combine. Divide salad among serving plates.

POMEGRANATE DRESSING Place ingredients in a screw-top jar; shake well.

TO REMOVE SEEDS FROM THE POMEGRANATE, CUT IT IN HALF CROSSWAYS; HOLD IT, CUT-SIDE DOWN, IN THE PALM OF YOUR HAND OVER A BOWL, THEN HIT THE OUTSIDE FIRMLY WITH A WOODEN SPOON. THE SEEDS SHOULD FALL OUT EASILY; DISCARD ANY WHITE PITH THAT FALLS OUT WITH THEM. POMEGRANATE MOLASSES IS AVAILABLE AT DELIS, MIDDLE-EASTERN FOOD STORES, SPECIALTY FOOD SHOPS AND MOST MAJOR SUPERMARKETS.

nutritional count per serving *47.1g total fat (10.3g saturated fat); 3503kJ (838 cal); 47.6g carbohydrate; 50.2g protein; 13.1g fibre*

BALSAMIC HONEY PULLED PORK BUNS

1 Preheat oven to 160°C/325°F.

2 Season pork. Heat oil in a large flameproof baking dish over high heat; cook pork 2 minutes each side or until browned. Add onion, garlic and herbs; cook, stirring, 2 minutes or until softened. Add stock and the water; bring to the boil. Cover; cook in oven for 2 hours. Remove the lid; cook a further 1 hour or until pork is tender.

3 Meanwhile, make cabbage and radish coleslaw.

4 Remove pork from dish, cover with foil; set aside. Strain cooking liquid into a medium bowl; discard solids. Reserve 1 cup of the cooking liquid.

5 Make balsamic honey barbecue sauce.

6 Shred pork then stir through barbecue sauce. Sandwich buns with shredded pork and coleslaw.

CABBAGE & RADISH COLESLAW Combine ingredients in a large bowl; season to taste. Refrigerate until required.

BALSAMIC HONEY BARBECUE SAUCE Heat oil in a large saucepan over medium heat; cook onion and garlic, stirring, until softened. Add remaining ingredients and reserved cooking liquid; bring to the boil. Reduce heat to low; simmer, uncovered, 15 minutes, stirring occasionally, or until reduced by half. Season to taste.

YOU COULD USE PORK SCOTCH FILLET (NECK) FOR THIS RECIPE.

PREP + COOK TIME 3 HOURS 45 MINUTES

MAKES 4

800G (1½-POUND) PIECE TRIMMED PORK SHOULDER

2 TABLESPOONS OLIVE OIL

1 LARGE BROWN ONION (200G), CHOPPED

4 CLOVES GARLIC

4 SPRIGS FRESH THYME

2 SPRIGS FRESH ROSEMARY

2 CUPS (500ML) CHICKEN STOCK

1 CUP (250ML) WATER

4 BRIOCHE BUNS (280G), SPLIT

CABBAGE & RADISH COLESLAW

200G (6½ OUNCES) CABBAGE, SLICED THINLY

4 TRIMMED RADISHES (60G), SLICED THINLY

2 TABLESPOONS FINELY CHOPPED FRESH CHIVES

¾ CUP (150G) MAYONNAISE

2 TABLESPOONS WHITE WINE VINEGAR

BALSAMIC HONEY BARBECUE SAUCE

3 TEASPOONS OLIVE OIL

1 SMALL BROWN ONION (80G), CHOPPED FINELY

2 CLOVES GARLIC, CRUSHED

1 CUP (250ML) BALSAMIC VINEGAR

½ CUP (140G) TOMATO SAUCE (KETCHUP)

¼ CUP (55G) FIRMLY PACKED BROWN SUGAR

2 TABLESPOONS HONEY

1 TABLESPOON WORCESTERSHIRE SAUCE

1 TABLESPOON DIJON MUSTARD

nutritional count per serving 30.9g total fat (5.1g saturated fat); 4130kJ (987 cal); 114.8g carbohydrate; 56.8g protein; 7.3g fibre

RISOTTO

BASIC RISOTTO

PREP + COOK TIME 35 MINUTES SERVES 4

1 LITRE (4 CUPS) CHICKEN STOCK

½ CUP (125ML) DRY WHITE OR RED WINE

¼ CUP (60ML) OLIVE OIL

100G (3 OUNCES) BUTTER, CHOPPED

1 SMALL BROWN ONION (80G), CHOPPED FINELY

2 CLOVES GARLIC, CRUSHED

1½ CUPS (300G) CARNAROLI OR ARBORIO RICE

½ CUP (40G) FINELY GRATED PARMESAN

1 Place stock and wine in a medium saucepan; bring to a simmer over medium heat and keep at a gentle simmer.
2 Heat oil and half the butter in a heavy-based medium saucepan over medium heat; cook onion and garlic, stirring, 5 minutes or until onion is soft. Add rice; stir 2 minutes or until well coated in oil. Stir in 1 cup hot stock mixture until liquid is absorbed. Continue adding stock mixture, 1 cup at a time, stirring frequently, until liquid is absorbed after each addition. Stir in remaining butter and the parmesan until melted. Serve immediately.

nutritional count per serving *38g total fat (17.4g saturated fat); 2697kJ (645 cal); 62g carbohydrate; 9.9g protein; 1g fibre*

24

FENNEL, LEMON & SCALLOP RISOTTO

PREP + COOK TIME 45 MINUTES SERVES 4

Make one quantity basic risotto (recipe page 24), omitting the parmesan. Heat 30g (1 ounce) butter in a frying pan over medium heat; cook 1 finely chopped bulb baby fennel 5 minutes or until tender. Season. Stir fennel mixture into risotto with finely grated rind of 1 lemon and 2 tablespoons finely chopped fresh chives. Heat 30g (1 ounce) butter in same frying pan over medium heat; cook 400g (12½ ounces) scallops, in batches, for 1 minute each side or until just tender. Serve risotto immediately, topped with scallops and fennel fronds.

RED WINE, PUMPKIN & ROSEMARY RISOTTO

PREP + COOK TIME 50 MINUTES SERVES 4

Make one quantity basic risotto (recipe page 24) with red wine. Preheat oven to 190°C/375°F. Cut 500g (1 pound) peeled seeded butternut pumpkin into 1cm (½-inch) pieces; toss with 1 tablespoon olive oil and 1½ teaspoons fresh rosemary leaves in a roasting pan. Season. Roast 35 minutes or until tender. Stir half the pumpkin mixture into risotto. Serve risotto immediately, topped with remaining pumpkin.

CABBAGE, PANCETTA & GORGONZOLA RISOTTO

PREP + COOK TIME 50 MINUTES SERVES 4

Make one quantity basic risotto (recipe page 24). Heat 1 tablespoon olive oil in a frying pan over medium heat; cook 150g (4½ ounces) pancetta cut into 6mm (¼-inch) pieces, stirring, 5 minutes. Stir in 400g (12½ ounces) shredded savoy cabbage (about ¼ cabbage); cook, covered, 10 minutes. Season. Stir cabbage mixture into risotto with 40g (1½ ounces) crumbled gorgonzola. Serve immediately, topped with fresh flat-leaf parsley leaves.

SMOKED SALMON, SPINACH & MASCARPONE RISOTTO

PREP + COOK TIME 45 MINUTES SERVES 4

Make one quantity basic risotto (recipe page 24), omitting the parmesan. Heat 1 tablespoon olive oil in a frying pan over medium heat; cook 2 thinly sliced green onions (scallions) and 1 cup baby spinach leaves, stirring, 2 minutes or until spinach is just wilted. Stir spinach mixture into risotto with 100g (3 ounces) thinly sliced smoked salmon. Spoon risotto into bowls, top with 100g (3 ounces) smoked salmon torn into pieces and a tablespoon of mascarpone. Sprinkle with 2 tablespoons chopped fresh dill. Serve immediately.

27

A TAGINE IS BOTH THE NAME OF THE DISH AND THE TRADITIONAL EARTHENWARE VESSEL WHICH IS USED FOR COOKING IT IN. THE VESSEL HAS A FLAT-BOTTOMED BASE AND A CONICAL LID, DESIGNED TO TRAP THE STEAM AND KEEP THE FOOD MOIST. AN ENAMELED CAST-IRON PAN WHICH HOLDS THE HEAT EVENLY IS A GOOD ALTERNATIVE.

MEATBALL TAGINE WITH EGGS

PREP + COOK TIME 1 HOUR

SERVES 4

500G (1 POUND) MINCED (GROUND) BEEF

1 CLOVE GARLIC, CRUSHED

¼ CUP FINELY CHOPPED FRESH MINT

2 TABLESPOONS FINELY CHOPPED FRESH CORIANDER (CILANTRO)

1 TEASPOON GROUND CINNAMON

1 TEASPOON GROUND CORIANDER

2 TEASPOONS GROUND CUMIN

½ TEASPOON CHILLI POWDER

1 TABLESPOON OLIVE OIL

1 MEDIUM BROWN ONION (150G), CHOPPED FINELY

4 LARGE TOMATOES (880G), CHOPPED COARSELY

PINCH SAFFRON THREADS

4 EGGS

½ CUP LOOSELY PACKED FRESH CORIANDER (CILANTRO) LEAVES

1 Combine beef, garlic, mint, chopped coriander, cinnamon, ground coriander, half the cumin and half the chilli in a large bowl; season. Roll level tablespoons of mixture into balls.

2 Heat oil in a tagine or large frying pan over medium heat; cook meatballs, in two batches, until browned. Remove from tagine.

3 Cook onion in same heated tagine, stirring, until softened. Add tomato, saffron and remaining cumin and chilli; bring to the boil. Reduce heat; simmer, uncovered, 15 minutes or until tomatoes soften.

4 Return meatballs to tagine; simmer, uncovered, 10 minutes or until meatballs are cooked and sauce thickens slightly. Season to taste. Carefully crack eggs into tagine; simmer, covered, 5 minutes or until whites of eggs are set and yolks remain runny. Sprinkle tagine with coriander leaves.

SERVING SUGGESTION Serve with pitta bread and Greek-style yoghurt.

nutritional count per serving *20.2g total fat (7.1g saturated fat); 1488kJ (356 cal); 6.6g carbohydrate; 35.3g protein; 3.5g fibre*

POACHED OCEAN TROUT WITH JAPANESE DRESSING

1 Place stock and the water in a medium saucepan; bring to the boil over medium heat. Reduce heat to a simmer, add fish fillets; cook 8 minutes or until almost cooked through. Using a slotted spoon, transfer fish to plate; cool 5 minutes.

2 Return poaching liquid to the boil, add asparagus and beans; cook 30 seconds or until asparagus is just tender. Drain. Refresh in iced water; drain.

3 Make japanese dressing.

4 Place sesame seeds in a small frying pan over medium heat; stir continuously 2 minutes or until golden. Remove from heat immediately.

5 Thinly slice radishes. Halve, seed and thinly slice cucumber diagonally. Place cucumber and radish in a large bowl; add spinach, mizuna and vegetables. Flake fish, add to salad; drizzle with the dressing. Divide salad among bowls. Sprinkle with sesame seeds to serve.

JAPANESE DRESSING Place ingredients in a small screw-top jar; shake well.

YOU CAN USE WATERCRESS AND TATSOI LEAVES INSTEAD OF THE BABY SPINACH AND MIZUNA, IF YOU LIKE. THIS RECIPE CAN BE PREPARED 8 HOURS AHEAD TO THE END OF STEP 4; STORE, COVERED, IN THE FRIDGE UNTIL YOU'RE READY TO ASSEMBLE.

PREP + COOK TIME 35 MINUTES

SERVES 6

1½ CUPS (375ML) FISH STOCK

2 CUPS (500ML) WATER

4 X 200G (6½-OUNCE) SKINLESS OCEAN TROUT FILLETS

340G (11 OUNCES) ASPARAGUS, CUT DIAGONALLY INTO SHORT LENGTHS

160G (5 OUNCES) GREEN BEANS, TRIMMED, CUT INTO 2CM (¾-INCH) LENGTHS

2 TABLESPOONS SESAME SEEDS

500G (1 POUND) SMALL RADISHES, TRIMMED

1 MEDIUM TELEGRAPH CUCUMBER (400G)

200G (6½ OUNCES) BABY SPINACH LEAVES

200G (6½ OUNCES) MIZUNA LEAVES

JAPANESE DRESSING

30G (1-OUNCE) PIECE FRESH GINGER, GRATED FINELY

¼ CUP (60ML) OLIVE OIL

2 TABLESPOONS LIME JUICE

¼ CUP (60ML) MIRIN

¼ CUP (60ML) SOY SAUCE

1 TABLESPOON FINELY GRATED PALM SUGAR

1 SMALL RED CHILLI, CHOPPED FINELY

nutritional count per serving *18.6g total fat (3.4g saturated fat); 1637kJ (391 cal); 11.7g carbohydrate; 40.3g protein; 4.9g fibre*

LAMB & LENTIL SALAD

PREP + COOK TIME 40 MINUTES

SERVES 6

1½ CUPS (300G) FRENCH-STYLE GREEN LENTILS

750G (1½ POUNDS) LAMB BACKSTRAPS

1 TABLESPOON OLIVE OIL

2 TEASPOONS GROUND CUMIN

350G (11 OUNCES) BABY GREEN BEANS, TRIMMED

1 SMALL RED ONION (100G), SLICED THINLY

1 CUP (110G) COARSELY CHOPPED ROASTED WALNUTS

2 CUPS FIRMLY PACKED FRESH FLAT-LEAF PARSLEY LEAVES

200G (6½ OUNCES) FETTA, CRUMBLED

POMEGRANATE DRESSING

⅓ CUP (80ML) OLIVE OIL

2 TABLESPOONS LEMON JUICE

1 TABLESPOON POMEGRANATE MOLASSES

2 TEASPOONS BROWN SUGAR

1 Cook lentils in a large saucepan of boiling water 15 minutes or until tender; drain.

2 Meanwhile, make pomegranate dressing.

3 Combine lentils with half the dressing in a large bowl.

4 Cook lamb on a heated oiled chargrill plate (barbecue or grill), brushing frequently with combined oil and cumin, for 4 minutes each side or until cooked as desired. Remove from heat, cover loosely with foil; rest for 5 minutes. Slice thickly.

5 Boil, steam or microwave beans until tender; drain. Refresh under cold water; drain.

6 Add beans to lentils with onion, nuts, parsley, fetta and remaining dressing; toss gently to combine. Serve lentil salad topped with lamb.

POMEGRANATE DRESSING Place ingredients in a screw-top jar, season to taste; shake well.

nutritional count per serving *41.3g total fat (10.2g saturated fat); 2880kJ (689 cal); 26.4g carbohydrate; 48.3g protein; 10.8g fibre*

POMEGRANATE MOLASSES IS AVAILABLE AT DELIS, MIDDLE-EASTERN FOOD STORES AND SPECIALTY FOOD SHOPS. YOU CAN USE RED WINE VINEGAR INSTEAD.

COOL EMPANADAS BEFORE PACKING INTO AIRTIGHT CONTAINERS; REFRIGERATE FOR UP TO 2 DAYS. EMPANADAS CAN ALSO BE FROZEN COOKED OR UNCOOKED. UNCOOKED EMPANADAS CAN BE BAKED FROM FROZEN. THAW BAKED EMPANADAS BEFORE REHEATING.

SPICY BEEF EMPANADAS

1 Cook 1 egg in a small saucepan of boiling water for 7 minutes or until hard boiled. Drain under cold water. When cool enough to handle, peel egg.

2 Meanwhile, boil, steam or microwave potato until tender. Drain; cool.

3 Heat oil in a large frying pan over medium heat; cook onion and garlic, stirring, 5 minutes or until soft. Add beef; cook, stirring, over high heat, until browned. Stir in spices; cook until fragrant. Add stock, paste, sultanas and potato; simmer, uncovered, for 3 minutes or until sauce thickens.

4 Meanwhile, coarsely chop boiled egg and olives; stir into beef mixture. Season. Cool.

5 Preheat oven to 200°C/400°F. Line two large oven trays with sheets of baking paper.

6 Using an 11 cm (4½-inch) round cutter, cut out 28 rounds from pastry. Place 1 rounded tablespoon of beef mixture in centre of each round; lightly brush edge with water. Fold in half to enclose filling, pinch edges to seal. Place empanadas, seam-side up, on trays; brush edges with remaining lightly beaten egg.

7 Bake empanadas for 30 minutes or until browned lightly.

SERVING SUGGESTION Serve with tomato chutney or sauce (ketchup).

YOU WILL NEED AN 11 CM (4½-INCH) ROUND PASTRY CUTTER FOR THIS RECIPE.

PREP + COOK TIME 1 HOUR 15 MINUTES

MAKES 28

2 EGGS

1 MEDIUM DESIREE POTATO (200G), CHOPPED FINELY

2 TEASPOONS OLIVE OIL

1 SMALL BROWN ONION (80G), CHOPPED FINELY

2 CLOVES GARLIC, CRUSHED

250G (8 OUNCES) MINCED (GROUND) BEEF

½ TEASPOON GROUND CUMIN

½ TEASPOON SMOKED PAPRIKA

¼ TEASPOON DRIED CHILLI FLAKES

½ CUP (125ML) BEEF STOCK

2 TEASPOONS TOMATO PASTE

2 TABLESPOONS SULTANAS

¼ CUP (30G) PITTED GREEN OLIVES

7 SHEETS SHORTCRUST PASTRY

nutritional count per empanada *13g total fat (6.5g saturated fat); 917kJ (219 cal); 20.1g carbohydrate; 5.2g protein; 1g fibre*

MINTED BEEF & RICE NOODLES

PREP + COOK TIME 30 MINUTES (+ REFRIGERATION)

SERVES 4

350G (11 OUNCES) BEEF RUMP STEAK, SLICED THINLY

6 CLOVES GARLIC, CRUSHED

2 TABLESPOONS FISH SAUCE

3 TEASPOONS MILD ASIAN CURRY POWDER

1 TEASPOON GRATED FRESH GINGER

200G (6½ OUNCES) RICE VERMICELLI NOODLES

2 MEDIUM CARROTS (240G)

½ MEDIUM DAIKON (300G)

1 SMALL LEBANESE CUCUMBER (130G)

8 MEDIUM LETTUCE LEAVES, SHREDDED

1 CUP (80G) BEAN SPROUTS, TRIMMED

1 TABLESPOON PEANUT OIL

¼ CUP FRESH MINT LEAVES

¼ CUP FRESH VIETNAMESE MINT LEAVES

¼ CUP FRESH CORIANDER (CILANTRO) LEAVES

¾ CUP (110G) UNSALTED ROASTED PEANUTS, CHOPPED

DRESSING

¼ CUP (60ML) LIME JUICE

¼ CUP (60ML) FISH SAUCE

1 SMALL FRESH RED CHILLI, SEEDED, CHOPPED FINELY

1 TEASPOON CASTER SUGAR (SUPERFINE SUGAR)

1 Combine beef, garlic, sauce, curry powder and ginger in a medium bowl. Cover; refrigerate 3 hours.

2 Place noodles in a heatproof bowl, cover with boiling water; stand 5 minutes. Drain.

3 Meanwhile, make dressing.

4 Cut carrots, daikon and cucumber into matchsticks. Place vegetables in a large bowl with lettuce and sprouts; toss gently to combine.

5 Heat oil in a wok or frying pan over high heat; stir-fry beef, in two batches, for 3 minutes or until beef is browned and just cooked though.

6 Add beef and noodles to vegetable mixture with herbs, nuts and dressing; toss gently to combine.

DRESSING Stir ingredients in a small bowl until sugar dissolves.

VIETNAMESE MINT IS AVAILABLE FROM ASIAN GROCERS AND SELECTED GREEN GROCERS. IT HAS A VERY DISTINCT TASTE, SO IF IT'S NOT AVAILABLE, REPLACE IT WITH THAI BASIL OR INCREASE THE QUANTITY OF MINT AND CORIANDER LEAVES SLIGHTLY.

nutritional count per serving *38g total fat (10.4g saturated fat); 2531kJ (605 cal); 21.8g carbohydrate; 40g protein; 9g fibre*

SALAD NIÇOISE

PREP + COOK TIME 45 MINUTES

SERVES 4

600G (1¼ POUNDS) BABY NEW POTATOES, HALVED

200G (6½ OUNCES) GREEN BEANS, TRIMMED, HALVED

2 X 200G (6½-OUNCE) THICK-CUT TUNA STEAKS

1 TABLESPOON OLIVE OIL

1 SMALL RED ONION (100G), SLICED THINLY

4 MEDIUM ROMA (EGG) TOMATOES (600G), SEEDED, SLICED

3 HARD-BOILED EGGS, QUARTERED

⅓ CUP (40G) PITTED SMALL BLACK OLIVES

⅓ CUP (55G) CAPERBERRIES, RINSED

¼ CUP FRESH MICRO BASIL LEAVES OR SMALL BASIL LEAVES

2 TABLESPOONS COARSELY CHOPPED FRESH FLAT-LEAF PARSLEY

DRESSING

⅓ CUP (80ML) OLIVE OIL

¼ CUP (60ML) WHITE WINE VINEGAR

1 TABLESPOON LEMON JUICE

1 SHALLOT (25G), CHOPPED FINELY

1 Place potatoes in a small saucepan, cover with cold water. Bring to the boil; cook for 15 minutes or until tender. Drain.

2 Meanwhile, boil, steam or microwave beans until tender; drain. Refresh under cold water; drain.

3 Make dressing.

4 Place hot potatoes in a large bowl with one-third of the dressing; toss gently to combine.

5 Brush tuna with oil; season. Heat a heavy-based frying pan over high heat; cook tuna for 1 minute each side for medium-rare or until cooked as desired. Cut into thin slices.

6 Add beans to bowl with onion, tomato, egg, olives, caperberries, herbs and remaining dressing; toss gently to combine. Serve salad topped with tuna.

DRESSING Place ingredients in a screw-top jar, season; shake well.

nutritional count per serving *32.5g total fat (6g saturated fat); 2843kJ (680 cal); 26.6g carbohydrate; 64.8g protein; 7.3g fibre*

TWICE-BAKED CHEESE SOUFFLÉS WITH GREENEST GREEN SALAD

PREP + COOK TIME 1 HOUR (+ COOLING)

SERVES 6

50G (1½ OUNCES) BUTTER, CHOPPED

⅓ CUP (50G) PLAIN (ALL-PURPOSE) FLOUR

1½ CUPS (375ML) MILK

1 CUP (120G) GRATED VINTAGE CHEDDAR

3 EGGS, SEPARATED

⅓ CUP (80ML) POURING CREAM

GREENEST GREEN SALAD

5 SLICES MULTI-GRAIN BREAD (180G)

150G (4½ OUNCES) GREEN BEANS, TRIMMED

170G (5½ OUNCES) ASPARAGUS, HALVED LENGTHWAYS IF LARGE

⅔ CUP (80G) FROZEN PEAS

½ CUP (130G) BASIL PESTO

1 TABLESPOON WATER

2 TABLESPOONS LEMON JUICE

3 CUPS (90G) LOOSELY PACKED TRIMMED WATERCRESS SPRIGS

1 MEDIUM RIPE AVOCADO (250G)

1 Preheat oven to 180°C/350°F. Grease six ⅔ cup (160ml) metal dariole moulds or soufflé dishes; line bases with baking paper.

2 Melt butter in a medium saucepan over medium heat, add flour; cook, stirring, 1 minute. Gradually stir in milk; stir until mixture boils and thickens. Transfer mixture to a medium heatproof bowl. Stir in ¾ cup of the cheddar, then egg yolks. Season to taste.

3 Beat egg whites in a small bowl with an electric mixer until soft peaks form. Fold egg white into cheese mixture, in two batches. Spoon mixture into moulds. Place moulds in a small baking dish; add enough boiling water to the baking dish to come halfway up side of the moulds.

4 Bake soufflés for 15 minutes or until firm. Stand in moulds for 5 minutes.

5 Turn soufflés out into a baking-paper-lined ovenproof dish. Spoon cream over soufflés; top with remaining cheddar. Bake further 15 minutes or until puffed and browned.

6 Meanwhile, make greenest green salad.

7 Divide salad into bowls, top with warm soufflés. Serve immediately.

GREENEST GREEN SALAD Toast bread; tear into bite-sized pieces. Place beans in a medium saucepan of boiling salted water; boil, uncovered, 1 minute. Add asparagus; boil 1½ minutes. Add peas; boil a further 30 seconds or until bright green. Drain; place in a large bowl of iced water to cool. Drain well. Place pesto in a large bowl; stir in the water and 1 tablespoon of the juice. Add bread, beans, asparagus and peas, then watercress; toss gently to coat. Season to taste. Halve avocado; scoop flesh into a small bowl, drizzle with remaining juice. Place on salad.

nutritional count per serving *41g total fat (17.7g saturated fat); 2356kJ (563 cal); 27.5g carbohydrate; 19g protein; 6g fibre*

SOUFFLÉS CAN BE BAKED THE FIRST TIME 8 HOURS AHEAD. BAKE FOR THE SECOND TIME JUST BEFORE SERVING. YOU WILL NEED A BUNCH OF WATERCRESS THAT WEIGHS ABOUT 350G (11 OUNCES).

PLOUGHMAN'S LUNCH

1 Make bread and butter pickles.

2 Preheat oven to 200°C/400°F. Line a large oven tray with baking paper.

3 Heat oil in a large frying pan; cook onion, stirring, over medium heat until soft. Add sugar and vinegar; cook, stirring occasionally, 10 minutes or until onion is caramelised. Cool.

4 Sift flours into a large bowl, add husks to bowl; rub in butter. Stir in half the cheddar and half the chives. Add egg and enough buttermilk to mix to a soft sticky dough. Turn dough onto a floured surface; knead gently until smooth.

5 Roll dough between sheets of baking paper into a 30cm x 40cm (12-inch x 16-inch) rectangle. Spread caramelised onion on dough leaving a 2cm (¾-inch) border along the far long side; top with remaining chedder and remaining chives. Roll up firmly from long side; transfer to tray.

6 Using a sharp knife, cut dough into eight slices, without cutting all the way through. Gently push slices to the left and right. Brush with a little extra buttermilk.

7 Bake bread for 40 minutes or until browned. Stand on tray 20 minutes before serving with pickles, ham, extra cheddar and celery.

BREAD & BUTTER PICKLES Combine cucumber and onion in a glass or stainless steel bowl; sprinkle with salt, mix well. Cover; stand 30 minutes. Rinse, then drain cucumber mixture; pat dry with paper towel. Spoon into a hot sterilised jar. Stir remaining ingredients in a medium saucepan over high heat, until sugar dissolves. Bring to the boil; remove from heat. Pour enough hot vinegar mixture into jar to cover cucumber mixture; seal immediately.

TIPS For information on sterilising jars, see page 141. Refrigerate pickles after opening. The cucumbers will lose their colour on standing.

PREP + COOK TIME 2 HOURS (+ COOLING & STANDING)

SERVES 8

2 TABLESPOONS OLIVE OIL

2 MEDIUM WHITE ONIONS (300G), SLICED THINLY

1 TABLESPOON BROWN SUGAR

2 TABLESPOONS BALSAMIC VINEGAR

3 CUPS (450G) SELF-RAISING FLOUR

1 CUP (160G) WHOLEMEAL SELF-RAISING FLOUR

100G (3 OUNCES) COLD BUTTER, CHOPPED

1 CUP (120G) COARSELY GRATED VINTAGE CHEDDAR

¼ CUP COARSELY CHOPPED FRESH CHIVES

1 EGG, BEATEN LIGHTLY

1¼ CUPS (310ML) BUTTERMILK, APPROXIMATELY

400G (12½ OUNCES) SLICED LEG HAM OFF THE BONE

200G (6 OUNCES) VINTAGE CHEDDAR, EXTRA

8 SMALL STALKS CELERY (600G)

BREAD & BUTTER PICKLES

250G (8 OUNCES) LEBANESE CUCUMBERS, UNPEELED, SLICED THINLY LENGTHWAYS

1 LARGE BROWN ONION (200G), SLICED THINLY

2 TABLESPOONS SEA SALT

½ CUP (125ML) RICE WINE VINEGAR

½ CUP (110G) WHITE (GRANULATED) SUGAR

1 TEASPOONS MUSTARD SEEDS

¼ TEASPOON DRIED CHILLI FLAKES

¼ TEASPOON GROUND TURMERIC

nutritional count per serving *33g total fat (18g saturated fat); 2817kJ (673 cal); 59g carbohydrate; 30g protein; 9g fibre*

THAI COCONUT-POACHED CHICKEN & HERB SALAD

PREP + COOK TIME 1 HOUR

SERVES 4

800ML CANNED COCONUT MILK

1 TABLESPOON COARSELY CHOPPED FRESH CORIANDER (CILANTRO) ROOT AND STEM

2 CLOVES GARLIC, SLICED THINLY

2 FRESH KAFFIR LIME LEAVES, SHREDDED FINELY

800G (1½ POUNDS) CHICKEN BREAST FILLETS

10CM (4-INCH) STICK FRESH LEMON GRASS (20G)

1 LEBANESE CUCUMBER (130G), HALVED LENGTHWAYS, SEEDED, SLICED THINLY

1½ CUPS (120G) BEAN SPROUTS

¾ CUP LOOSELY PACKED FRESH CORIANDER (CILANTRO) LEAVES

½ CUP LOOSELY PACKED FRESH MINT LEAVES

1 FRESH LONG RED CHILLI, SLICED THINLY

CORIANDER & LIME DRESSING

2 TEASPOONS COARSELY CHOPPED FRESH CORIANDER (CILANTRO) ROOT AND STEM

2 CLOVES GARLIC

2 FRESH SMALL RED CHILLIES

1 TABLESPOON CASTER SUGAR (SUPERFINE SUGAR)

¼ CUP (60ML) LIME JUICE

2 TEASPOONS FISH SAUCE

1 Combine coconut milk, coriander root and stem mixture, garlic and lime leaves in a large saucepan; bring to the boil. Add chicken; return to the boil. Reduce heat; simmer, uncovered, 10 minutes or until chicken is almost cooked through. Remove from heat; stand chicken in poaching liquid 10 minutes. Remove chicken from liquid; when cool enough to handle, shred coarsely.

2 Reserve 1 cup of the poaching liquid; discard remainder. Place reserved poaching liquid in same pan; bring to the boil. Boil for 10 minutes or until reduced by two-thirds. Add shredded chicken; cool 10 minutes.

3 Meanwhile, make coriander and lime dressing.

4 Place lemon grass in a small heatproof bowl, cover with boiling water; soak 5 minutes or until just tender. Drain; slice thinly.

5 Place lemon grass in a large bowl with cucumber, sprouts, herbs, chilli and dressing; toss gently to combine. Divide chicken mixture into bowls; top with salad.

CORIANDER & LIME DRESSING Using a mortar and pestle, pound coriander root and stem mixture, garlic, chillies and sugar to a paste. Add juice and fish sauce; stir until sugar dissolves.

nutritional count per serving *52.7g total fat (39.7g saturated fat); 3056kJ (731 cal); 13.9g carbohydrate; 48.7g protein; 6g fibre*

SPICY MEXICAN SOUP WITH CHICKEN

1 Bring a medium saucepan of water to the boil. Cut a shallow cross in the base of each tomato, then add to water; boil 30 seconds. Drain; place in a bowl of iced water. Peel then discard skin. Chop tomatoes.

2 Trim celery; coarsely chop leaves, reserve ⅓ cup. Coarsely chop stalk.

3 Heat oil in a large saucepan over low heat; cook onion, carrot, celery, coriander stem and spices, stirring, for 8 minutes or until vegetables are softened. Add tomato; cook, stirring, until soft. Add the water, then chicken; bring to the boil. Reduce heat; simmer, covered, 45 minutes or until chicken is very tender.

4 Meanwhile, combine coriander leaves, chilli and reserved celery leaves in a small bowl.

5 Remove chicken from soup; cool slightly. Shred chicken, then return to soup with juice; season to taste. Stir over medium heat until hot.

6 Serve soup topped with chilli mixture.

PREP + COOK TIME 1 HOUR 15 MINUTES

SERVES 4

3 LARGE ROMA (EGG) TOMATOES (270G)

½ CELERY STALK (75G), LEAVES ON

1 TABLESPOON VEGETABLE OIL

½ MEDIUM RED ONION (85G), CHOPPED FINELY

1 SMALL CARROT (70G), CHOPPED

1 TABLESPOON FINELY CHOPPED FRESH CORIANDER (CILANTRO) STEM

1 TEASPOON SMOKED PAPRIKA

½ TEASPOON GROUND CUMIN

½ TEASPOON GROUND CORIANDER

1 LITRE (4 CUPS) WATER OR SALT-REDUCED CHICKEN STOCK

500G (1 POUND) CHICKEN THIGH FILLETS

⅓ CUP COARSELY CHOPPED FRESH CORIANDER (CILANTRO)

⅓ CUP (80G) COARSELY CHOPPED PICKLED JALAPEÑO CHILLI

¼ CUP (60ML) LIME JUICE

nutritional count per serving *27.9g total fat (7.5g saturated fat); 1510kJ (361 cal); 4.9g carbohydrate; 21.2g protein; 2.8g fibre*

GREEN VEGETABLE PIE WITH YELLOW SPLIT PEA DIP

PREP + COOK TIME 1 HOUR 15 MINUTES (+ STANDING)

SERVES 8

250G (8 OUNCES) ZUCCHINI, SLICED VERY THINLY

1 TEASPOON SALT

780G (1½ POUNDS) SILVER BEET (SWISS CHARD)

200G (6½ OUNCES) GREEN BEANS, TRIMMED

125G (4 OUNCES) GREEK FETTA, CRUMBLED

125G (4 OUNCES) KEFALOTYRI CHEESE OR PARMESAN, GRATED

¼ CUP CHOPPED FRESH FLAT-LEAF PARSLEY

2 TABLESPOONS CHOPPED FRESH DILL

1 TABLESPOON CHOPPED FRESH MINT

¾ CUP (50G) STALE BREADCRUMBS

6 EGGS, BEATEN LIGHTLY

¼ CUP (35G) SESAME SEEDS, TOASTED

1 TABLESPOON OLIVE OIL

8 SMALL ROUNDS PITTA BREAD, WARMED

2 MEDIUM LEMONS (280G), CUT INTO WEDGES

YELLOW SPLIT PEA DIP

1 CUP (200G) DRIED YELLOW SPLIT PEAS

1 SMALL ONION (80G), CHOPPED

4 CLOVES GARLIC, BRUISED

1 TEASPOON GROUND CUMIN

1 TEASPOON GROUND CORIANDER

⅓ CUP (80ML) EXTRA VIRGIN OLIVE OIL

¼ CUP (60ML) LEMON JUICE

1 Preheat oven to 180°C/350°F. Oil a 24cm (9½-inch) springform pan; line base with baking paper.

2 Combine zucchini and salt in a colander over a bowl; stand 30 minutes. Rinse zucchini under cold water; pat dry with paper towel. Trim stems from silver beet; discard stems. You will need 300g (9½ ounces) leaves.

3 Meanwhile, cook beans in a large saucepan of boiling, salted water for 5 minutes or until tender. Remove beans, then plunge into a bowl of iced water; drain well. Finely chop beans.

4 Add silver beet to water in pan, return to the boil; drain immediately. Cool under running water; drain again. Squeeze silver beet to remove excess moisture, then pat dry with paper towel. Finely chop silver beet.

5 Place zucchini, beans and silver beet in a large bowl and combine well with cheeses, herbs, breadcrumbs, egg, sesame seeds and oil; season. Spoon mixture into pan; smooth surface.

6 Bake pie 35 minutes or until set and golden. Stand in pan 15 minutes.

7 Meanwhile, make yellow split pea dip.

8 Serve pie warm or at room temperature cut into wedges with dip, pitta bread and lemon wedges. Top with extra parsley, if you like.

YELLOW SPLIT PEA DIP Place split peas in a small saucepan with enough cold water to just cover; bring to the boil. Drain; rinse. Return peas to pan with onion and garlic, add enough cold water to cover by 6cm (2½ inches); bring to the boil. Reduce heat to medium; simmer for 25 minutes or until peas are tender and beginning to collapse. Drain. Cool to room temperature. Process split pea mixture and spices until smooth. With motor operating, gradually add oil in a steady stream, then add juice in a steady stream. Season to taste. (Makes about 2¼ cups.)

nutritional count per serving *28.3g total fat (8.9g saturated fat); 2736kJ (653 cal); 64.6g carbohydrate; 30.7g protein; 8.8g fibre*

KEFALOTYRI IS A SEMI-FIRM GREEK SHEEP'S OR GOAT'S MILK CHEESE. ALTHOUGH CALLED A PIE, THIS TRADITIONAL GREEK VEGETABLE-AND-HERB-PACKED RECIPE CONTAINS NO PASTRY AND IS HELD TOGETHER WITH EGGS AND FETTA.

TO SAVE TIME, YOU CAN BUY SHELLED PRAWNS FROM THE FISHMONGER. THE TORTILLA STRIPS CAN BE PREPARED A DAY AHEAD; COOL, THEN STORE IN AN AIRTIGHT CONTAINER.

CHARGRILLED PRAWN & CORN SALAD

1 Peel and devein prawns, leaving tails intact. Combine prawns, garlic, juice, cumin, sugar and oil in a large bowl. Cover; refrigerate 10 minutes.

2 Meanwhile, make dressing.

3 Brush corn with butter; season. Cook corn on a heated oiled chargrill pan (or barbecue), turning, 10 minutes or until browned lightly and just tender. Using a sharp knife, cut kernels from cobs. Place in a small bowl; cover to keep warm.

4 Meanwhile, heat extra oil in a medium frying pan over medium heat; fry tortilla strips, in two batches, stirring, 2 minutes or until golden. Remove with a slotted spoon; drain on paper towel. Season with salt to taste.

5 Season prawn mixture; cook on heated chargrill pan for 3 minutes, turning halfway, or until just cooked through.

6 Place lettuce, radish, avocado and three-quarters of the coriander in a large bowl; toss gently to combine. Arrange lettuce mixture on a platter; layer with prawns and corn, then drizzle with dressing.

7 Serve salad topped with tortilla strips and remaining coriander.

DRESSING Place ingredients in a screw-top jar, season; shake well.

PREP + COOK TIME 50 MINUTES

SERVES 4

20 UNCOOKED MEDIUM KING PRAWNS (SHRIMP) (1KG)

2 CLOVES GARLIC, CRUSHED

2 TABLESPOONS LIME JUICE

½ TEASPOON GROUND CUMIN

1 TEASPOON CASTER SUGAR (SUPERFINE SUGAR)

1 TABLESPOON OLIVE OIL

2 TRIMMED CORN COBS (500G)

20G (¾ OUNCE) BUTTER, SOFTENED

2 TABLESPOONS OLIVE OIL, EXTRA

3 X 15CM (6-INCH) CORN TORTILLAS, CUT INTO THIN STRIPS

½ MEDIUM ICEBERG LETTUCE (120G), SHREDDED FINELY

6 SMALL RADISHES (100G), TRIMMED, SLICED VERY THINLY

1 MEDIUM AVOCADO (250G), SLICED

1 CUP LOOSELY PACKED FRESH CORIANDER (CILANTRO) LEAVES

DRESSING

2 TABLESPOONS LIME JUICE

¼ CUP (60ML) OLIVE OIL

1 FRESH LONG GREEN CHILLI, SEEDED, CHOPPED FINELY

1 CLOVE GARLIC, CRUSHED

1 TEASPOON CASTER SUGAR (SUPERFINE SUGAR)

nutritional count per serving *43.9g total fat (9.6g saturated fat); 2619kJ (626 cal); 21g carbohydrate; 32.3g protein; 9g fibre*

SLOW
DINNERS

CHEESE RAVIOLI WITH SILVER BEET & PEPPERONI

PREP + COOK TIME 45 MINUTES

SERVES 6

1KG (2 POUNDS) SILVER BEET (SWISS CHARD), TRIMMED, CHOPPED COARSELY

150G (4½ OUNCES) BUTTER, CHOPPED

150G (4½ OUNCES) PEPPERONI, CHOPPED COARSELY

2 CLOVES GARLIC, SLICED THINLY

¼ CUP (40G) CURRANTS

¼ CUP (60ML) LEMON JUICE

50G (1½ OUNCES) PECORINO CHEESE OR PARMESAN, SHAVED

900G (1¾ POUNDS) THREE-CHEESE RAVIOLI

¼ CUP FRESH SAGE LEAVES

⅔ CUP (90G) ROASTED HAZELNUTS, CHOPPED COARSELY

1 Place silver beet in a large saucepan of boiling water, stir until just wilted; drain well.

2 Heat 50g (1½ ounces) butter in a large frying pan until golden; cook pepperoni, stirring until slightly crisp. Add garlic and currants; cook until garlic is lightly golden. Add silver beet and 1 tablespoon of the juice; toss to combine. Reduce heat to low; cook, covered, for 5 minutes or until silver beet is heated through and tender. Season to taste. Remove from heat; stand 2 minutes. Add pecorino; toss gently to combine.

3 Meanwhile, cook ravioli in a large saucepan of boiling salted water until just tender; drain. Return ravioli to pan, add silver beet mixture; toss to combine. Divide into bowls.

4 Wipe frying pan clean; heat remaining butter in pan until it begins to foam. Stir in sage; cook 2 minutes or until butter begins to brown. Add nuts and remaining juice. Season to taste. Spoon butter mixture immediately over ravioli.

YOU CAN USE ANY VEGETABLE- OR CHEESE-FILLED RAVIOLI OR TORTELLINI IF YOU PREFER. YOU CAN USE SALAMI OR PANCETTA INSTEAD OF THE PEPPERONI.

nutritional count per serving *47.3g total fat (21.4g saturated fat); 3052kJ (729 cal); 47g carbohydrate; 23.5g protein; 5.6g fibre*

SPRINGFORM PANS AND PIE TINS AREN'T ALWAYS MADE FROM THE BEST MATERIALS FOR BROWNING PASTRY ON A PIE. TO HELP THE BROWNING PROCESS, PLACE THE PIE ON A PREHEATED OVEN TRAY, AND TURN YOUR OVEN TO ITS FAN FUNCTION FOR THE LAST 15 MINUTES OF COOKING.

CHICKEN & TARRAGON PIE WITH POLENTA CRUST

1 Make polenta pastry.

2 Meanwhile, heat half the oil in a large frying pan over medium heat; cook chicken, in batches, until browned. Drain on paper towel. Heat remaining oil in same pan; cook leek and kumara, stirring, 3 minutes. Add wine and stock; cook, stirring occasionally, for 10 minutes, or until most of the liquid has evaporated. Remove from heat; stir in chicken, combined crème fraîche and flour, then tarragon. Cool.

3 Cut pastry in half. Roll out one half on a floured work surface until large enough to line a deep 23cm (9¼-inch) springform pan or deep pie tin. Ease pastry into pan; press into base and side. Cover; refrigerate 1 hour.

4 Preheat oven to 200°C/400°F; heat an oven tray.

5 Spoon chicken mixture into pastry case; brush pastry edge with a little of the reserved egg mixture. Roll out remaining pastry on a floured work surface until large enough to cover filling. Lift pastry onto filling; press pastry together to join. Trim edge, then press to seal with a fork. Brush top of pie with remaining reserved egg mixture; sprinkle with polenta.

6 Place pie on hot tray; bake 20 minutes. Reduce oven to 180°C/350°F; bake a further 25 minutes or until pastry is golden. Stand pie in pan for 10 minutes before serving.

POLENTA PASTRY Process sifted flour, polenta and butter until mixture resembles breadcrumbs. Combine egg and the water; reserve 1 tablespoon for brushing. Add remaining egg mixture to flour mixture, process until pastry begins to come together. Turn onto a work surface; knead lightly into a ball. Wrap in plastic wrap; refrigerate 2 hours.

SERVING SUGGESTION Serve with mixed green peas and beans.

PREP + COOK TIME 1 HOUR 40 MINUTES (+ REFRIGERATION)

SERVES 6

2 TABLESPOONS OLIVE OIL

1KG (2 POUNDS) CHICKEN THIGH FILLETS, CUT INTO 3CM (1¼-INCH) PIECES

1 LARGE LEEK (500G), WHITE PART ONLY, CHOPPED COARSELY

1 KUMARA (ORANGE SWEET POTATO) (400G), CHOPPED COARSELY

½ CUP (125ML) DRY WHITE WINE

½ CUP (125ML) CHICKEN STOCK

200G (6½ OUNCES) CRÈME FRAÎCHE

1 TABLESPOON PLAIN (ALL-PURPOSE) FLOUR

2 TEASPOONS FINELY CHOPPED FRESH TARRAGON

2 TEASPOONS POLENTA

POLENTA PASTRY

2 CUPS (300G) PLAIN (ALL-PURPOSE) FLOUR

½ CUP (80G) POLENTA

200G (6½ OUNCES) UNSALTED COLD BUTTER, CHOPPED

2 EGGS, BEATEN LIGHTLY

¼ CUP (60ML) ICE-COLD WATER

nutritional count per serving *79.7g total fat (37g saturated fat); 4732kJ (1130 cal); 62g carbohydrate; 38g protein; 5.4g fibre*

FIVE-SPICE PORK WITH GREEN ONION BREAD

PREP + COOK TIME 3 HOURS (+ REFRIGERATION)

SERVES 12

1 LARGE TOMATO (220G), CHOPPED

2 TABLESPOONS TOMATO PASTE

2 FRESH SMALL RED CHILLIES, SEEDED, CHOPPED COARSELY

3 TEASPOONS GROUND STAR ANISE

3 TEASPOONS GROUND CINNAMON

1 TEASPOON GROUND FENNEL SEEDS

¼ TEASPOON GROUND CLOVES

6 CLOVES GARLIC

4 TEASPOONS GRATED FRESH GINGER

¼ CUP (60ML) SOY SAUCE

1½ TABLESPOONS FISH SAUCE

½ CUP (110G) FIRMLY PACKED BROWN SUGAR

2KG (4 POUNDS) BONELESS PORK BELLY, RIND REMOVED, FAT TRIMMED

230G (7 OUNCES) BABY CORN

¼ CUP (60ML) SESAME OIL

1 CUP (280G) CHINESE PLUM SAUCE

GREEN ONION BREAD

20 GREEN ONIONS (SCALLIONS), SLICED

1 CUP CORIANDER (CILANTRO) LEAVES

½ CUP FINELY CHOPPED GARLIC CHIVES

4 CUPS (600G) PLAIN (ALL-PURPOSE) FLOUR

4 TEASPOONS BAKING POWDER

2 TEASPOONS SALT

2 TABLESPOONS SESAME OIL

4 TEASPOONS CHILLI OIL

1⅓ CUPS (330ML) WARM WATER

PEANUT OIL, FOR SHALLOW-FRYING

1 Process fresh tomato and paste, chilli, spices, garlic, ginger, sauces and sugar until it forms a paste. Place pork in a glass or ceramic dish, add paste; turn pork to coat. Cover; refrigerate 1 hour.

2 Preheat oven to 180°C/350°F.

3 Line a roasting pan with foil; fit with an oiled roasting rack. Remove pork from marinade (reserve marinade); place, fat-side down, on rack in pan. Roast 30 minutes. Turn pork, brushing with a little reserved marinade; roast 1 hour, basting every 15 minutes. Roast a further 30 minutes, without basting, until top is dark and crisp. Cool.

4 Meanwhile, make green onion bread.

5 Combine baby corn and oil in a small bowl; season to taste. Cook on a heated chargrill plate (or barbecue) until corn is lightly charred and just cooked.

6 Serve sliced pork with plum sauce, baby corn and green onion bread.

GREEN ONION BREAD Combine green onion, coriander and chives; set aside. Process sifted flour, baking powder and salt until combined. Add combined oils and the water, pulse until mixture just comes together. Turn out onto work surface; shape dough into a ball. Wrap in plastic wrap; refrigerate 15 minutes. Divide dough in half, roll each half into a 36cm (14½-inch) log; cut each log into 12 pieces. Place pieces, cut-side down, on a board (cover pieces with plastic wrap until ready to use). Roll pieces, in batches, on a lightly floured surface until 15cm (6-inch) round; top with green onion mixture, pressing lightly into dough. Roll up like a swiss roll, then form roll into a spiral. Flatten spiral; roll out until 12cm (4¾-inches) round. Heat 3mm (⅛-inch) peanut oil in a frying pan over medium heat; fry rounds, in batches, for 1½ minutes each side or until golden, adding more oil as necessary. (Makes 24)

nutritional count per serving *29g total fat (7.6g saturated fat); 2943kJ (703 cal); 66.7g carbohydrate; 40.9g protein; 6.2g fibre*

A SEAFOOD BISQUE HAS A DEEP LUXURIOUS SEAFOOD FLAVOUR. THIS COMES FROM COOKING PRAWNS IN THEIR SHELLS, AS WELL AS FISH FILLETS, INTO A STOCK. IT IS THEN BLENDED (SHELLS AND ALL) INTO A SMOOTH, SILKY SOUP.

SEAFOOD BISQUE

1 Shell and devein 8 prawns, keeping tails intact; place shells and heads in a large bowl. Reserve shelled prawns in a small bowl; cover, refrigerate, until required. Add remaining unshelled prawns to large bowl.

2 Heat half the oil in a large saucepan over high heat; cook onion, garlic, carrot and celery, stirring, for 5 minutes or until onion begins to soften. Add prawn mixture; cook, stirring 5 minutes or until prawns change colour. Stir in herbs and paste. Add the water and wine; bring to the boil. Reduce heat to medium-low, add fish; simmer 20 minutes, skimming the surface occasionally with a ladle to remove scum.

3 Remove fish from stock; cover until required.

4 Increase stock to medium heat, add tomatoes and potatoes; season. Cook for 40 minutes or until soup has reduced slightly. Cool 10 minutes.

5 Blend soup, in batches, until smooth. Push blended soup through a fine sieve into a clean medium saucepan over heat; return to the boil.

6 Meanwhile, heat remaining oil in a large frying pan over medium-high heat; cook reserved prawns for 1 minute each side or until just cooked through.

7 Stir crème fraîche and juice into soup; season to taste. Ladle soup into bowls; top with flaked fish, prawns and extra chopped parsley.

PREP + COOK TIME 2 HOURS

SERVES 8

1.5KG (3 POUNDS) UNCOOKED LARGE KING PRAWNS (SHRIMP)

2 TABLESPOONS OLIVE OIL

1 MEDIUM BROWN ONION (150G), CHOPPED COARSELY

2 CLOVES GARLIC, CRUSHED

1 MEDIUM CARROT (120G), CHOPPED

1 CELERY STALK (150G), CHOPPED

6 SPRIGS FRESH THYME

¼ CUP LOOSELY PACKED FRESH FLAT-LEAF PARSLEY

2 TABLESPOONS TOMATO PASTE

2 LITRES (8 CUPS) WATER

½ CUP (125ML) DRY WHITE WINE

800G (1½ POUNDS) FIRM WHITE FISH FILLETS, SKINNED

400G (12½ OUNCES) CANNED CRUSHED TOMATOES

3 MEDIUM POTATOES (600G), CHOPPED

½ CUP (120G) CRÈME FRAÎCHE

⅓ CUP (80ML) LEMON JUICE

2 TABLESPOONS CHOPPED FRESH FLAT-LEAF PARSLEY, EXTRA

nutritional count per serving *12.7g total fat (5g saturated fat); 1459kJ (348 cal); 12.6g carbohydrate; 41.7g protein; 3.7g fibre*

SLOW-ROASTED LAMB LEG WITH SOFT POLENTA

PREP + COOK TIME 5 HOURS 45 MINUTES

SERVES 6

3KG (6-POUND) LEG OF LAMB

1 WEDGE PRESERVED LEMON

2 MEDIUM BROWN ONIONS (300G), CHOPPED COARSELY

4 CLOVES GARLIC, CHOPPED

600G (1½ POUNDS) CANNED CHOPPED TOMATOES

¼ CUP (70G) TOMATO PASTE

3 BAY LEAVES

¼ CUP (40G) CURRANTS

¼ CUP (60ML) RED WINE

1 TEASPOON GROUND CORIANDER

1 TEASPOON GROUND CUMIN

1 TEASPOON GROUND GINGER

¼ TEASPOON LOOSELY PACKED SAFFRON THREADS

¼ TEASPOON GROUND CLOVES

¼ TEASPOON GROUND CARDAMOM

¼ TEASPOON GROUND CINNAMON

2 TABLESPOONS OLIVE OIL

⅓ CUP (45G) SLIVERED ALMONDS

¾ CUP LOOSELY PACKED FRESH CORIANDER (CILANTRO) LEAVES

80G (2½ OUNCES) PERSIAN FETTA

SOFT POLENTA

1 LITRE (4 CUPS) MILK

1 CLOVE GARLIC, BRUISED

¾ CUP (120G) POLENTA

1 Preheat oven to 160°C/325°F.

2 Trim excess fat from lamb, if necessary. Pull away flesh from preserved lemon; discard flesh. Rinse rind well, then chop finely. Combine rind with onion, garlic, tomatoes, tomato paste, bay leaves, currants and wine in a large oven bag. Combine spices in a small bowl. Rub oil all over lamb, then spice mixture; place lamb in oven bag. Place lamb in bag on a large oven tray. Seal the bag using the tie provided, then pierce five or six times near the top of the bag to allow steam to escape during cooking. Roast 5 hours or until lamb is very tender.

3 Half an hour before serving, make soft polenta.

4 Meanwhile, place nuts in a single layer on an oven tray; roast 8 minutes or until browned.

5 Pull meat from lamb leg in large chunks. Divide polenta among shallow bowls, top with meat and remaining sauce. Sprinkle with nuts, coriander and drained fetta.

SOFT POLENTA Bring milk and garlic almost to the boil in a large saucepan. Gradually add polenta, whisking continuously. Stir over medium heat for 10 minutes or until thickened; discard garlic. Season with salt. (Stir in extra milk if required to make a soft consistency.)

TIP You will need 1 large oven bag for this recipe.

nutritional count per serving *91.2g total fat (27g saturated fat); 5342kJ (1276 cal); 36.3g carbohydrate; 76g protein; 5.2g fibre*

THE SALSA CAN BE PARTIALLY PREPARED UP TO A DAY AHEAD — ADD THE PARSLEY, EXTRA VIRGIN OLIVE OIL AND LEMON JUICE JUST BEFORE YOU START TO COOK THE FISH.

PAN-FRIED WHITING WITH LEEK, TOMATO & OLIVE SALSA

1 Make leek, tomato and olive salsa.

2 Place potatoes in a large saucepan, cover with cold water; bring to the boil. Boil for 8 minutes or until tender; drain. Transfer to a large bowl; drizzle with vinegar and 1 tablespoon of the oil. Cover to keep warm.

3 Meanwhile, cook green beans in a saucepan of boiling salted water for 3 minutes or until tender; drain. Refresh in iced water; drain. Add to potatoes in bowl; toss gently to combine.

4 Season flour with salt and pepper; coat fish in seasoned flour, shake off excess. Heat remaining oil in a large frying pan over medium heat; cook fish, skin-side down, in batches, 1½ minutes or until skin crisps. Turn, cook a further 1 minute or until just cooked through.

5 Divide potato and beans among plates; top with fish and salsa.

LEEK, TOMATO & OLIVE SALSA Heat olive oil in a medium saucepan over medium heat; cook leek, stirring occasionally, for 5 minutes or until softened. Add garlic; cook, stirring, until fragrant. Stir in tomatoes, olives and capers; cook until heated through. Remove from heat; stir in parsley, extra virgin olive oil and juice. Season to taste.

PREP + COOK TIME 50 MINUTES

SERVES 6

1KG (2 POUNDS) KIPFLER (FINGERLING) POTATOES, CUT LENGTHWAYS

2 TABLESPOONS WHITE WINE VINEGAR

¼ CUP (60ML) OLIVE OIL

400G (12½ OUNCES) GREEN BEANS, TRIMMED

½ CUP (75G) PLAIN (ALL-PURPOSE) FLOUR

12 X 80G (2½-OUNCE) WHITING FILLETS, SKIN ON

LEEK, TOMATO & OLIVE SALSA

2 TABLESPOONS OLIVE OIL

2 MEDIUM LEEKS (700G), TRIMMED, SLICED THINLY

2 CLOVES GARLIC, CRUSHED

500G (1 POUND) GRAPE TOMATOES, HALVED

150G (4½ OUNCES) SICILIAN GREEN OLIVES

2 TABLESPOONS DRAINED CAPERS, RINSED

1 CUP FIRMLY PACKED FRESH FLAT-LEAF PARSLEY LEAVES

¼ CUP (60ML) EXTRA VIRGIN OLIVE OIL

2 TABLESPOONS LEMON JUICE

nutritional count per serving *32.7g total fat (5.2g saturated fat); 2668kJ (637 cal); 33.5g carbohydrate; 46.5g protein; 9.3g fibre*

65

CHINESE-BRAISED VEAL

PREP + COOK TIME 5 HOURS 15 MINUTES

SERVES 6

2.2KG (4¾ POUNDS) CUBED VEAL SHOULDER (OR OTHER STEWING CUT)

1¾ CUPS (350G) MEDIUM-GRAIN RICE

500G (1 POUND) BABY BUK CHOY

2 TEASPOONS SESAME OIL

1 TABLESPOON TOASTED SESAME SEEDS

¼ CUP (60ML) RICE WINE VINEGAR

¼ CUP (55G) CASTER SUGAR (SUPERFINE SUGAR)

2 GREEN ONIONS (SCALLIONS), SLICED THICKLY

¼ CUP FRESH CORIANDER (CILANTRO) LEAVES

CHINESE STOCK

1 MEDIUM ORANGE (240G)

8 GREEN ONIONS (SCALLIONS), HALVED

10 CLOVES GARLIC, HALVED

75G (2½-OUNCE) PIECE FRESH GINGER, SLICED THINLY LENGTHWAYS

1½ CUPS (375ML) LIGHT SOY SAUCE

1.5 LITRES (6 CUPS) WATER

2 CUPS (500ML) CHINESE COOKING WINE (SHAO HSING)

10 STAR ANISE

4 CINNAMON STICKS

1 TEASPOON SESAME OIL

1 Preheat oven to 160°C/325°F.

2 Make chinese stock.

3 Add veal to chinese stock; bring to a simmer over low heat. Transfer to oven; cook, covered, 4½ hours or until meat is very tender.

4 Strain mixture over a large heatproof bowl; reserve braising liquid. Remove and discard whole spices and rind from veal mixture; reserve veal.

5 Line another strainer with paper towel; place over another heatproof bowl. Add reserved braising liquid to strainer a ladleful at a time, changing paper as needed until you have 1.75 litres (7 cups) clarified (clear) stock. Reserve 1½ cups for this recipe (freeze remaining stock for another use). The stock will taste quite salty at this stage but will be balanced in flavour once the vinegar and sugar are added in step 7.

6 Cook rice according to directions on packet. Steam or microwave buk choy; toss in sesame oil and seeds while hot.

7 Meanwhile, place reserved clarified stock with vinegar and sugar in a large frying pan over high heat; bring to the boil. Boil for 10 minutes or until syrupy. Reduce heat, add reserved veal; cook, stirring, until veal is well coated in dark syrupy mixture.

8 Serve rice, buk choy and veal in bowls, topped with green onion and coriander.

CHINESE STOCK Using a vegetable peeler, peel wide strips of rind from orange. Combine rind with remaining ingredients in a large casserole.

nutritional count per serving *30.8g total fat (13.9g saturated fat); 4579kJ (1094 cal); 56.5g carbohydrate; 144g protein; 3.6g fibre*

YOU CAN STRAIN THE STOCK THROUGH A
PIECE OF MUSLIN OR A CLEAN OPEN WEAVE
CLOTH INSTEAD OF THE PAPER TOWEL.

LAMB SHANK & BEAN RAGÙ

1 Place dried beans in a large bowl, cover with cold water; soak 8 hours or overnight.

2 Drain soaked beans, rinse under cold water; drain. Place beans in a medium saucepan, cover with water; bring to the boil. Reduce heat; simmer, uncovered, for 15 minute (beans will not be fully cooked at this stage). Drain.

3 Preheat oven to 180°C/350°F.

4 Place flour in a medium bowl; season with salt and pepper. Toss lamb in flour; shake away excess. Heat half the oil in a large casserole over medium heat; cook lamb, in batches, turning until browned all over. Remove from dish. Wipe dish clean if necessary.

5 Heat remaining oil in dish over medium heat; cook onion, carrot, celery, garlic and chilli, stirring, for 5 minutes or until onion softens.

6 Return lamb to dish with beans, vinegar, tomatoes, anchovies, cinnamon, rosemary, wine and the water; bring to the boil. Cover with a lid; cook in oven, 1 hour, turning shanks halfway through cooking. Uncover; cook a further 1 hour or until meat is almost falling off the bone.

7 Just before serving, stir parsley through ragù.

SERVING SUGGESTION Serve with polenta or mashed potato.

YOU NEED TO SOAK THE DRIED BEANS FOR 8 HOURS AT THE START OF THIS RECIPE.

PREP + COOK TIME 3 HOURS (+ STANDING)

SERVES 4

½ CUP (100G) DRIED HARICOT BEANS

½ CUP (100G) DRIED BORLOTTI BEANS

2 TABLESPOONS PLAIN (ALL-PURPOSE) FLOUR

8 FRENCH-TRIMMED LAMB SHANKS (2.4KG)

2 TABLESPOONS OLIVE OIL

1 LARGE BROWN ONION (200G), CHOPPED

1 MEDIUM CARROT (120G), CHOPPED

1 STALK CELERY (150G), TRIMMED, CHOPPED COARSELY

2 CLOVES GARLIC, CRUSHED

1 FRESH LONG RED CHILLI, CHOPPED FINELY

¼ CUP (60ML) BALSAMIC VINEGAR

400G (12½ OUNCES) CANNED CRUSHED TOMATOES

8 ANCHOVIES

1 CINNAMON STICK

2 SPRIGS FRESH ROSEMARY

½ CUP (125ML) RED WINE

2 CUPS (500ML) WATER

⅓ CUP FRESH FLAT-LEAF PARSLEY SPRIGS

nutritional count per serving 33.8g total fat (8.4g saturated fat); 2732kJ (653 cal); 17.4g carbohydrate; 60.4g protein; 15.6g fibre

ONLY THE RIND OF PRESERVED LEMON IS USED. REMOVE THE FLESH FROM THE WEDGE BY PULLING IT AWAY FROM THE RIND; DISCARD THE FLESH. RINSE THE RIND WELL BEFORE USING. WE USED BRINE-CURED SICILIAN OLIVES FOR THEIR LOVELY BUTTERY FLAVOUR AND TEXTURE, BUT YOU COULD USE KALAMATA OLIVES INSTEAD.

ROAST CHICKEN WITH OLIVES & PRESERVED LEMON

PREP + COOK TIME 1 HOUR 30 MINUTES (+ REFRIGERATION)

SERVES 6

2 WEDGES PRESERVED LEMON

6 CLOVES GARLIC, CRUSHED

1½ TEASPOONS GROUND GINGER

1 TEASPOON GROUND CUMIN

1 TEASPOON SWEET PAPRIKA

1 TEASPOON CHILLI FLAKES

½ TEASPOON GROUND TURMERIC

2 TABLESPOONS OLIVE OIL

6 CHICKEN MARYLANDS (2KG)

¼ TEASPOON SAFFRON THREADS

1 CUP (250ML) BOILING WATER

4 MEDIUM BROWN ONIONS (600G), SLICED THINLY

150G (4½ OUNCES) PITTED SICILIAN GREEN OLIVES

1 CUP LOOSELY PACKED FRESH CORIANDER (CILANTRO) LEAVES

1 Remove flesh from preserved lemon; discard flesh. Rinse rind well. Finely chop rind of 1 wedge; thinly slice rind of the other wedge. Combine chopped rind, garlic, spices and half the oil in a large bowl with chicken. Cover; refrigerate 3 hours or overnight.

2 Preheat oven to 180°C/350°F.

3 Combine saffron and the water in a small heatproof bowl.

4 Heat remaining oil in a large frying pan; cook chicken, in batches, until browned both sides. Remove from pan.

5 Cook onion in same pan for 5 minutes or until softened. Add saffron mixture; bring to the boil. Spread onion mixture over the base of a large shallow ovenproof dish; arrange chicken on top, in a single layer.

6 Roast chicken for 35 minutes. Add thinly sliced rind and olives; roast a further 25 minutes or until chicken is cooked through.

7 Just before serving chicken, top with coriander.

SERVING SUGGESTION Serve with steamed Israeli couscous mixed with coarsely chopped fresh flat-leaf parsley.

nutritional count per serving *23.3g total fat (5.2g saturated fat); 1790kJ (428 cal); 6g carbohydrate; 46.3g protein; 3.8g fibre*

HONEY-ROASTED CHICKEN WITH SPICY FRIED POTATOES

1 Preheat oven to 200°C/400°F.

2 Rinse chicken under cold water; pat dry inside and out with paper towel. Tuck wings under chicken; tie legs together with kitchen string.

3 Combine honey, oil, garlic, spices and oregano in a small bowl. Place chicken in a medium oiled roasting pan; rub honey mixture over chicken. Pour the water into the pan, add lemon; season.

4 Roast chicken 1 hour, covering any parts that are overbrowning with oiled foil, or until juices run clear when a skewer is inserted into the thickest part of a thigh.

5 Meanwhile, make spicy fried potatoes.

6 Serve honey-roasted chicken with spicy fried potatoes.

SPICY FRIED POTATOES Place potatoes in a large saucepan, add enough cold water to just cover; bring to the boil. Boil for 6 minutes or until almost tender (cooking time will vary depending on the size of the potatoes). Drain; leave to cool and dry completely in a colander. About 15 minutes before chicken is cooked, heat oil in a large frying pan; cook potatoes, paste, garlic and seeds, turning occasionally, for 15 minutes or until potatoes are browned. Stir in rind and parsley; season to taste.

SERVING SUGGESTION Serve with kohlrabi, cabbage and parmesan salad (recipe page 86).

PREP + COOK TIME 1 HOUR 30 MINUTES

SERVES 4

1.6KG (3¼-POUND) WHOLE CHICKEN

2 TABLESPOONS HONEY, WARMED

1 TABLESPOON EXTRA VIRGIN OLIVE OIL

2 CLOVES GARLIC, CRUSHED

½ TEASPOON GROUND CUMIN

½ TEASPOON GROUND CORIANDER

¼ TEASPOON GROUND CINNAMON

½ TEASPOON SWEET PAPRIKA

2 TEASPOONS CHOPPED FRESH OREGANO

½ CUP (125ML) WATER

1 MEDIUM LEMON (280G), HALVED

SPICY FRIED POTATOES

1KG (2 POUNDS) BABY NEW POTATOES, HALVED

2 TABLESPOONS OLIVE OIL

1 TABLESPOON HARISSA PASTE

2 CLOVES GARLIC, CRUSHED

2 TEASPOONS CUMIN SEEDS

2 TEASPOONS FINELY GRATED LEMON RIND

2 TABLESPOONS FINELY CHOPPED FRESH FLAT-LEAF PARSLEY

nutritional count per serving *38.5g total fat (9.6g saturated fat); 3106kJ (742 cal); 46.7g carbohydrate; 49.3g protein; 5.3g fibre*

SCOTCH FILLET, RIB-EYE, PORTERHOUSE (BONE-IN SIRLOIN), T-BONE AND RUMP ARE ALL SUITABLE STEAKS FOR THIS RECIPE. THIS RECIPE MAKES 1.25 LITRES (5 CUPS) OF KETCHUP. STORE IN THE FRIDGE FOR UP TO 3 MONTHS.

STEAK WITH SLOW-ROASTED TOMATO & JALAPEÑO KETCHUP

PREP + COOK TIME 3 HOURS (+ COOLING)

SERVES 6

1.5KG (3 POUNDS) POTATOES

¼ CUP (60ML) OLIVE OIL

6 X 220G (7-OUNCE) NEW YORK STEAKS (BONELESS SIRLOIN)

1 TABLESPOON CRACKED BLACK PEPPER

2 TABLESPOONS OLIVE OIL, EXTRA

SLOW-ROASTED TOMATO & JALAPEÑO KETCHUP

2 LARGE BROWN ONIONS (400G), QUARTERED

6 CLOVES GARLIC

1.5KG (3 POUNDS) TOMATOES, QUARTERED

2 FRESH JALAPEÑO CHILLIES, HALVED

2 TEASPOONS CUMIN SEEDS

2 TABLESPOONS OLIVE OIL

½ CUP (125ML) RED WINE VINEGAR

¾ CUP (165G) FIRMLY PACKED BROWN SUGAR

1 TABLESPOON SEA SALT FLAKES

1 Make slow-roasted tomato and jalapeño ketchup.

2 Preheat oven to 220°C/425°F.

3 Peel potatoes; slice thinly lengthways, then cut into thin chips. Combine potato and oil in a large bowl; season. Place chips, in a single layer, on a large oven tray. Roast 45 minutes or until dark golden and crisp.

4 Meanwhile, combine steaks, pepper and extra oil in a large bowl. Cook steaks on a heated oiled barbecue (chargrill plate or grill) for 2 minutes each side for medium rare or until cooked as desired.

5 Serve steaks and chips with ketchup.

SLOW-ROASTED TOMATO & JALAPEÑO KETCHUP Preheat oven to 180°C/350°F. Line two large oven trays with baking paper. Combine onion, garlic, tomatoes, jalapeño, cumin seeds and oil in a large bowl; place, in a single layer, on trays. Roast 1½ hours. Process mixture, in batches, until smooth. Pour mixture into a large saucepan with vinegar, sugar and salt; bring to a simmer over medium heat. Simmer 20 minutes or until sauce has reduced and thickened. Season to taste. Cool to room temperature.

SERVING SUGGESTION Serve with rocket (arugula).

nutritional count per serving *38.6g total fat (10.1g saturated fat); 4139kJ (989 cal); 67.1g carbohydrate; 88g protein; 9.4g fibre*

YOU CAN MAKE THE LAMB RAGÙ A DAY AHEAD. WHEN LAMB IS COOL ENOUGH TO HANDLE, SHRED THE MEAT INTO PIECES USING TWO FORKS. STIR THE SHREDDED MEAT INTO THE COOKING SAUCE. STORE IN THE FRIDGE UNTIL READY TO USE. REHEAT RAGÙ AS INSTRUCTED IN STEP 5.

LAMB RAGÙ MOUSSAKA

1 Make lamb ragù.

2 Preheat oven to 240°C/475°F.

3 Cut eggplants lengthways into medium-thick slices. Spray each side with cooking-oil spray. Place on wire racks on oven trays. Roast 10 minutes or until soft and brown at edges. Remove from oven. Reduce oven to 200°C/400°F.

4 Meanwhile, melt butter in a medium saucepan over medium heat, add flour; stir until mixture bubbles. Gradually pour in milk, whisking continuously until mixture boils and thickens. Add ½ cup (40g) of the parmesan, stir until melted. Remove from heat.

5 Remove lamb from oven bag; shred meat. Place cooking sauce from oven bag in a large saucepan over low heat, add shredded meat; stir ragù until heated through. Season to taste.

6 Combine breadcrumbs, rind, thyme and remaining parmesan in a medium bowl.

7 Grease a 24cm x 32cm x 6.5cm deep (9½-inch x 12¾-inch x 2¾-inch) (3.5-litre/14-cup capacity) ovenproof dish. Place half the eggplant slices in the dish, then top with half the ragù and half the white sauce. Repeat layering. Cover white sauce with breadcrumb mixture.

8 Bake moussaka for 35 minutes or until golden and heated through.

LAMB RAGÙ Preheat oven to 160°C/325°F. Trim excess fat from lamb, if necessary. Combine onion, garlic, tomatoes, paste, bay leaves, and wine in a large oven bag. Combine spices in a small bowl. Rub oil over lamb, then spice mixture; place lamb in oven bag. Place lamb in bag on a large oven tray. Seal the bag using the tie provided, then pierce five or six times near the top of the bag to allow steam to escape during cooking. Roast 4 hours or until lamb is very tender. Discard bay leaves.

PREP + COOK TIME 5 HOURS

SERVES 8

3 MEDIUM EGGPLANTS (960G)

COOKING-OIL SPRAY

80G (2½ OUNCES) BUTTER, CHOPPED

½ CUP (75G) PLAIN (ALL-PURPOSE) FLOUR

1 LITRE (4 CUPS) MILK

1¼ CUPS (100G) GRATED PARMESAN

¾ CUP (60G) PANKO (JAPANESE) BREADCRUMBS

2 TEASPOONS FINELY GRATED LEMON RIND

2 TEASPOONS FRESH THYME LEAVES

LAMB RAGÙ

2KG (4-POUND) BONELESS LEG OF LAMB

2 MEDIUM BROWN ONIONS (300G), CHOPPED COARSELY

4 CLOVES GARLIC, CHOPPED COARSELY

600G (1½ POUNDS) CANNED CHOPPED TOMATOES

¼ CUP (70G) TOMATO PASTE

3 BAY LEAVES

½ CUP (125ML) RED WINE

1 TEASPOON GROUND CORIANDER

1 TEASPOON GROUND CUMIN

2 TABLESPOONS OLIVE OIL

nutritional count per serving *82g total fat (27.5g saturated fat); 4547kJ (1086 cal); 27.7g carbohydrate; 56.8g protein; 6g fibre*

SLOW-COOKER SMOKY STICKY PORK RIBS WITH COLESLAW

PREP + COOK TIME 4 HOURS 45 MINUTES

SERVES 4

2KG (4 POUNDS) AMERICAN-STYLE PORK RIBS

3 CLOVES GARLIC, CRUSHED

1 CUP (280G) BARBECUE SAUCE

¼ CUP (60ML) LEMON JUICE

¼ CUP (55G) FIRMLY PACKED BROWN SUGAR

2 TEASPOONS SWEET SMOKED PAPRIKA

1 TEASPOON TABASCO SAUCE

COLESLAW

¼ SMALL GREEN CABBAGE (300G), SHREDDED FINELY

¼ SMALL RED CABBAGE (300G), SHREDDED FINELY

1 LARGE CARROT (180G), GRATED

½ SMALL RED ONION (50G), SLICED THINLY

1 CUP (120G) COARSELY GRATED VINTAGE CHEDDAR

2 TABLESPOONS CHOPPED FRESH CHIVES

¾ CUP (225G) MAYONNAISE

¼ CUP (60ML) CIDER VINEGAR

1 Cut pork ribs into pieces that will fit into the slow cooker.

2 Combine garlic with remaining ingredients in a large shallow dish; add pork, turn to coat pork in sauce. Transfer pork and sauce to a 4.5-litre (18-cup) slow cooker. Cook, covered, on high, for 4 hours. Turn ribs once during cooking time for even cooking.

3 When almost ready to serve, make coleslaw.

4 Carefully remove ribs from the cooker; cover to keep warm. Transfer sauce to a medium frying pan; bring to the boil. Reduce heat; simmer, skimming fat from surface, for 10 minutes or until sauce has reduced to 1 cup.

5 Serve ribs drizzled with sauce, and with coleslaw.

COLESLAW Place ingredients in a large bowl; toss gently to combine. Season to taste.

nutritional count per serving *57.1g total fat; 19.7g saturated fat; 4592kJ (1097 cal); 64g carbohydrate; 80g protein; 6.9g fibre*

ASK THE BUTCHER TO CUT THE RIBS INTO PIECES
THAT WILL FIT INTO YOUR SLOW COOKER.

THERE ARE DIFFERENT TYPES OF RISOTTO RICE, EACH ABSORBS LIQUID DIFFERENTLY. TAKE CARE WITH ARBORIO AS IT IS EASILY OVERCOOKED, WHILE CARNAROLI IS MUCH MORE FORGIVING.

OSSO BUCO WITH SAFFRON RISOTTO

1 Preheat oven to 170°C/340°F.

2 Place flour in a bowl; season with salt and pepper. Coat osso buco in flour; shake off excess. Heat oil in a large casserole over high heat; cook 2 minutes each side or until browned. Remove from pan.

3 Cook onion in same pan, stirring over medium-high heat, for 5 minutes or until softened. Add garlic, tomato, bay leaves and wine; bring to the boil. Reduce heat; simmer 2 minutes. Add stock, herbs and the water; return osso buco to pan, stirring well to combine. Bring to the boil. Cover with a lid; cook in oven 2 hours, turning osso buco halfway through cooking time, or until almost falling off the bone.

4 Half an hour before osso buco is cooked, make saffron risotto.

5 Meanwhile, make gremolata.

6 Spoon risotto into bowls, top with osso buco. Sprinkle with gremolata.

SAFFRON RISOTTO Combine saffron and wine in a small bowl; stand 5 minutes. Heat stock and the water in a medium saucepan. Melt half the butter in a large saucepan over medium heat; cook onion 5 minutes or until softened. Add rice; stir 1 minute to coat in mixture. Add wine mixture; cook, stirring, 3 minutes or until liquid is almost evaporated. Stir in 1 cup of hot stock mixture; cook, stirring, over low heat until liquid is absorbed. Continue adding stock mixture in 1-cup batches, stirring until liquid is absorbed after each addition. Cook 25 minutes or until all stock has been absorbed and rice is tender. Remove from heat; stir in parmesan and remaining butter. Season to taste.

GREMOLATA Remove rind from lemons with a zester, into thin strips. Combine ingredients in a small bowl.

TIP If you don't have a zesting tool, remove the rind thinly with a vegetable peeler then cut each piece into long, thin strips.

PREP + COOK TIME 2 HOURS 45 MINUTES

SERVES 8

1 CUP (150G) PLAIN (ALL-PURPOSE) FLOUR

8 X 3CM (1¼-INCH) THICK VEAL OSSO BUCO (2KG)

¼ CUP (60ML) OLIVE OIL

2 MEDIUM ONIONS (300G), CHOPPED FINELY

2 CLOVES GARLIC, CRUSHED

4 MEDIUM TOMATOES (600G), GRATED COARSELY, SKIN DISCARDED

2 BAY LEAVES

1 CUP (250ML) DRY WHITE WINE

2 CUPS (500ML) CHICKEN STOCK

2 TEASPOONS EACH FINELY CHOPPED FRESH SAGE, ROSEMARY AND THYME

1 CUP (250ML) WATER

SAFFRON RISOTTO

½ TEASPOON SAFFRON THREADS

¾ CUP (180ML) DRY WHITE WINE

3 CUPS (750ML) CHICKEN STOCK

3 CUPS (750ML) WATER

90G (3 OUNCES) BUTTER

1 LARGE ONION (200G), CHOPPED FINELY

2¼ CUPS (450G) ARBORIO OR CARNAROLI RISOTTO RICE

¾ CUP (60G) FINELY GRATED PARMESAN

GREMOLATA

2 MEDIUM LEMONS (280G)

½ CUP FINELY CHOPPED FRESH FLAT-LEAF PARSLEY

1 CLOVE GARLIC, CRUSHED

nutritional count per serving *24.2g total fat (10.2g saturated fat); 3429kJ (819 cal); 64g carbohydrate; 76.8g protein; 4g fibre*

SPICED LAMB ROAST WITH FIGS & HONEY

PREP + COOK TIME 1 HOUR 50 MINUTES

SERVES 6

3 CLOVES GARLIC, CHOPPED FINELY

4 TEASPOONS FINELY GRATED GINGER

2 FRESH LONG RED CHILLIES, CHOPPED FINELY

⅓ CUP FINELY CHOPPED FRESH CORIANDER (CILANTRO)

⅓ CUP FINELY CHOPPED FRESH FLAT-LEAF PARSLEY

2 TEASPOONS GROUND CUMIN

2 TEASPOONS GROUND CORIANDER

¼ CUP (60ML) OLIVE OIL

2KG (4-POUND) LEG OF LAMB

9 MEDIUM BLACK FIGS (540G), HALVED

2 TABLESPOONS HONEY

1 Preheat oven to 180°C/350°F.

2 Combine garlic, ginger, chilli, herbs, spices and oil in a small bowl.

3 Rub herb mixture all over lamb; season. Place lamb in an oiled large roasting pan; roast, uncovered, 1¼ hours.

4 Add figs to pan; drizzle honey over figs and lamb. Roast for a further 15 minutes or until lamb is cooked to medium or as desired. Cover lamb loosely with foil; rest 10 minutes.

5 Serve sliced lamb with figs.

TIP Make double the herb rub mixture; toss half the quantity through steamed couscous and serve with the lamb.

SERVING SUGGESTION Serve with couscous and a spinach salad.

nutritional count per serving *24.3g total fat (8.4g saturated fat); 2115kJ (506 cal); 15.6g carbohydrate; 55.6g protein; 2.9g fibre*

PAPPARDELLE WITH SAFFRON TOMATO & PRAWNS

1 Shell and devein prawns, leaving tails intact.

2 Heat half the oil in a large, heavy-based saucepan over medium heat; cook onion, garlic, celery, fennel, thyme and rind, stirring occasionally, for 10 minutes. Add saffron, chilli flakes and tomato paste; cook, stirring 5 minutes. Add wine; cook until liquid has almost evaporated. Add the water; simmer gently 15 minutes or until vegetables are tender. Add tomato; cook until heated through. Stir in juice. Season to taste.

3 Meanwhile, cook pasta in a large saucepan of boiling water until almost tender; drain. Transfer pasta to a large bowl, add sauce; toss gently to combine.

4 Heat a large frying pan over high heat until very hot, add 1½ tablespoons of the oil and half the prawns; toss 2 minutes or until just cooked through. Transfer to a bowl. Repeat with remaining oil and prawns.

5 Serve pasta mixture topped with prawns and parsley.

PREP + COOK TIME 1 HOUR 15 MINUTES

SERVES 8

2KG (4 POUNDS) UNCOOKED EXTRA LARGE PRAWNS (SHRIMP)

½ CUP (125ML) OLIVE OIL

1 LARGE ONION (200G), CHOPPED FINELY

4 CLOVES GARLIC, CHOPPED FINELY

4 STALKS CELERY (600G), TRIMMED, CHOPPED FINELY

3 BULBS BABY FENNEL (390G), TRIMMED, CHOPPED FINELY

2 TEASPOONS CHOPPED FRESH THYME LEAVES

1 TEASPOON GRATED ORANGE RIND

¾ TEASPOON SAFFRON THREADS

⅓ TEASPOON CHILLI FLAKES

¼ CUP (70G) TOMATO PASTE

¾ CUP (180ML) DRY WHITE WINE

3 CUPS (750ML) WATER

8 VERY RIPE MEDIUM VINE-RIPENED TOMATOES (1.2KG), PEELED, SEEDED, CHOPPED COARSELY

¼ CUP (60ML) LEMON JUICE

600G (1¼ POUNDS) DRIED PAPPARDELLE

¼ FRESH COARSELY CHOPPED FRESH FLAT-LEAF PARSLEY

TO REMOVE SKIN FROM TOMATOES, CUT A SMALL CROSS INTO THE BASE OF EACH TOMATO THEN PLUNGE, IN BATCHES, INTO A SAUCEPAN OF BOILING WATER FOR 15 SECONDS. REMOVE WITH A SLOTTED SPOON AND PLUNGE INTO A BOWL OF ICED WATER TO COOL. DRAIN, THEN PEEL AWAY SKINS.

nutritional count per serving   *16.4g total fat (2.7g saturated fat); 2308kJ (551 cal); 58.6g carbohydrate; 36g protein; 5.6g fibre*

SALADS

KOHLRABI, CABBAGE & PARMESAN SALAD

PREP TIME 20 MINUTES SERVES 6 AS A SIDE

Trim and cut 2 medium kohlrabi (730g) into matchsticks, finely shred ¼ medium savoy cabbage (225g) and coarsely chop ¾ cup loosely packed flat-leaf parsley leaves; combine in a large bowl. Add ⅓ cup coarsely chopped roasted skinless hazelnuts and 30g (1 ounce) shaved parmesan. Whisk ¼ cup extra virgin olive oil and 1 tablespoon red wine vinegar in a small bowl until combined; season to taste. Pour dressing over salad; toss gently to combine. Top with 30g (1 ounce) extra shaved parmesan.

COS HEARTS WITH GREEN GODDESS DRESSING

PREP + COOK TIME 20 MINUTES SERVES 4 AS A SIDE

Blend or process ½ medium avocado, 2 tablespoons whole-egg mayonnaise, 2 tablespoons chopped fresh chervil, 1 tablespoon chopped fresh chives, 1 small chopped shallot, ¼ cup water and 1 tablespoon extra virgin olive oil until smooth; season to taste. Heat 1 teaspoon olive oil to a large non-stick frying pan over high heat; cook 10 slices prosciutto, in batches, 1 minute each side or until crisp; drain on paper towel. Quarter 2 baby cos lettuce hearts lengthways, arrange on a platter; coarsely crumble crisp prosciutto over, then drizzle with dressing. Scatter with ¼ cup extra fresh chervil leaves.

COBB SALAD

PREP + COOK TIME 30 MINUTES SERVES 4 AS A MAIN

Whisk 1 tablespoon dijon mustard, 2½ tablespoons extra virgin olive oil and ¼ cup red wine vinegar in a small bowl; season to taste. Quarter 300g (7 ounces) kipfler potatoes lengthways; boil, steam or microwave until tender. Toss warm potatoes with 2 tablespoons of the dressing and 2 teaspoons finely chopped fresh chives; season to taste. Combine 1 cup tightly packed watercress with 1 teaspoon dressing. Arrange watercress, 125g (4 ounces) crumbled blue cheese, 2 cups (350g) shredded cooked chicken, 1 large thickly sliced avocado, 125g (4 ounces) halved grape tomatoes, 3 halved hard-boiled eggs and potato mixture in rows on a large platter. Drizzle with remaining dressing.

ROCKET, PEAR & RICOTTA FRITTER SALAD

**PREP + COOK TIME 30 MINUTES
SERVES 4 AS A LIGHT LUNCH OR SIDE**

Boil, steam or microwave ¾ cup frozen peas until tender; refresh under cold water. Combine 200g (7 ounces) ricotta, ¼ cup finely grated pecorino and ¼ cup self-raising flour in a medium bowl; season. Roll level teaspoons of ricotta mixture into balls; press into 4cm (1½-inches) discs. Heat 1 tablespoon olive oil in a large non-stick frying pan over medium heat; cook ricotta fritters, in two batches, for 1 minute each side or until golden. Drain on paper towel. Whisk ¼ cup lemon juice and 1½ tablespoons extra virgin olive oil in a small bowl; season to taste. Combine 1 thinly sliced pear with peas, 125g (4 ounces) rocket, ¼ cup tightly packed small fresh mint leaves and ¼ cup shaved pecorino and half the fritters; add dressing, toss to combine. Serve topped with remaining fritters.

SPINACH, PESTO & PARMESAN LASAGNE

PREP + COOK TIME 1 HOUR 15 MINUTES (+ STANDING)

SERVES 8

2 LARGE RED CAPSICUMS (BELL PEPPERS) (700G)

¼ CUP (60ML) OLIVE OIL

4 LARGE ZUCCHINI (600G), SLICED THINLY LENGTHWAYS

2 MEDIUM EGGPLANT (600G), SLICED THINLY LENGTHWAYS

6 FRESH LASAGNE SHEETS (300G)

150G (4½ OUNCES) BABY SPINACH LEAVES

⅔ CUP (50G) FINELY GRATED PARMESAN

BÉCHAMEL SAUCE

60G (2 OUNCES) BUTTER

¼ CUP (35G) PLAIN (ALL-PURPOSE) FLOUR

3 CUPS (750ML) MILK

½ CUP (40G) FINELY GRATED PARMESAN

PESTO

⅓ CUP (50G) PINE NUTS, ROASTED

2 CLOVES GARLIC, QUARTERED

1½ CUPS FIRMLY PACKED FRESH BASIL LEAVES

½ CUP (125ML) OLIVE OIL

1 Preheat oven to 200°C/400°F. Oil a deep 3-litre (12-cup) ovenproof dish.

2 Quarter capsicums; discard seeds and membranes, then slice thickly.

3 Heat a little of the olive oil in a large frying pan over medium heat; cook capsicum, zucchini and eggplant, separately, in batches, adding more oil as necessary until browned both sides. Season vegetables.

4 Make béchamel sauce, then pesto.

5 Layer zucchini in dish; top with one-third of the pesto, two lasagne sheets and one-third of the béchamel sauce. Repeat layering, replacing vegetable layer with eggplant, then capsicum and spinach. Sprinkle with cheese.

6 Bake lasagne, covered with foil, for 40 minutes. Remove foil; bake a further 15 minutes or until browned. Stand 10 minutes before serving.

BÉCHAMEL SAUCE Melt butter in a medium saucepan over medium heat, add flour; cook, stirring, until mixture bubbles. Gradually stir in milk; stir until mixture boils and thickens. Remove from heat; stir in cheese. Season to taste.

PESTO Process pine nuts, garlic and basil until finely chopped. With motor operating, gradually add oil in a thin, steady stream until combined. Season to taste.

SERVING SUGGESTION Serve with a rocket and pear salad.

nutritional count per serving *38.9g total fat (11.8g saturated fat); 2164kJ (517 cal); 26.5g carbohydrate; 13.4g protein; 6.2g fibre*

YOU COULD MAKE THE LASAGNE TO TAKE TO WORK DURING THE WEEK, SIMPLY FREEZE IT IN INDIVIDUAL SERVES IN AIRTIGHT CONTAINERS FOR UP TO 1 MONTH. THAW OVERNIGHT IN THE FRIDGE; REHEAT IN THE MICROWAVE AT WORK.

CHILLI PRAWN SKEWERS WITH KOSHUMBIR

1 Make koshumbir.

2 Shell and devein prawns, leaving tails intact. Thread four prawns onto each skewer.

3 Process spices, green chilli, coconut, ginger, nuts, coconut milk and oil until mixture forms a paste. Transfer to a small bowl; stir in the water.

4 Rub paste over prawns; cook skewers on a heated oiled chargrill plate (or barbecue or grill), brushing occasionally with remaining paste, until prawns are changed in colour and just cooked.

5 Serve skewers topped with coriander leaves, and koshumbir.

KOSHUMBIR Peel cucumber, then cut in half lengthways; scoop out seeds with a teaspoon. Cut cucumber and carrot into matchsticks or use an Asian vegetable stripper. Place cucumber and carrot in a medium bowl with remaining ingredients; toss gently to combine.

SERVING SUGGESTION Serve with naan, roti or other flat bread.

KOSHUMBIR, SOMETIMES SPELLED KOSHAMBIR, IS A FRESH SHREDDED VEGETABLE SALAD THAT IS SERVED IN INDIA ALONGSIDE CURRIES.

PREP + COOK TIME 1 HOUR

SERVES 4

32 UNCOOKED LARGE KING PRAWNS (2.2KG) (SHRIMP)

1 TEASPOON GROUND TURMERIC

1 TEASPOON CUMIN SEEDS

1 TABLESPOON CORIANDER SEEDS

¼ TEASPOON CHILLI FLAKES

2 FRESH LONG GREEN CHILLIES, CHOPPED

2 TABLESPOONS DESICCATED COCONUT

2 TEASPOONS FINELY GRATED GINGER

2 TABLESPOONS ROASTED ALMONDS

2 TABLESPOONS PISTACHIOS, ROASTED

½ CUP (125ML) CANNED COCONUT MILK

1 TABLESPOON VEGETABLE OIL

1 TABLESPOON WARM WATER

2 TABLESPOONS FRESH CORIANDER (CILANTRO) LEAVES

KOSHUMBIR

1 LEBANESE CUCUMBER (130G)

1 SMALL CARROT (70G)

1 SMALL BROWN ONION (80G), CHOPPED FINELY

1 FRESH LONG GREEN CHILLI, SEEDED, CHOPPED FINELY

3 TEASPOONS FINELY GRATED GINGER

¼ CUP (35G) ROASTED PEANUTS

1 TABLESPOON LEMON JUICE

nutritional count per serving *20.8g total fat (8g saturated fat); 1960kJ (468 cal); 6.2g carbohydrate; 61.6g protein; 4.5g fibre*

BEEF CURRY WITH COCONUT RICE

PREP + COOK TIME 1 HOUR 30 MINUTES (+ STANDING)

SERVES 6

2 TABLESPOONS PEANUT OIL

800G (1½ POUNDS) BEEF STRIPS

1 MEDIUM ONION (150G), CHOPPED FINELY

3 CLOVES GARLIC, CRUSHED

1 FRESH LONG RED CHILLI, SEEDED, CHOPPED FINELY

10CM (4-INCH) STALK FRESH LEMON GRASS (20G), CHOPPED FINELY

1 STAR ANISE

1 CINNAMON STICK, HALVED

4 CARDAMOM PODS, BRUISED

350G (11 OUNCES) SNAKE BEANS, CUT IN 4CM (1½-INCH) LENGTHS

2 TABLESPOONS GROUND BEAN SAUCE

2 TABLESPOONS FISH SAUCE

½ CUP FRESH CORIANDER (CILANTRO) LEAVES

COCONUT RICE

1¾ CUPS (350G) JASMINE RICE

400ML (12½ OUNCES) CANNED COCONUT CREAM

½ TEASPOON GROUND TURMERIC

1¼ CUPS (310ML) WATER

CRISP COCONUT & PEANUT TOPPING

2 TABLESPOONS PEANUT OIL

2 CLOVES GARLIC, CRUSHED

4 GREEN ONIONS (SCALLIONS), CHOPPED

3 CUPS (150G) FLAKED COCONUT

2 TABLESPOONS BROWN SUGAR

½ CUP (150G) TAMARIND CONCENTRATE

10CM (4-INCH) STALK FRESH LEMON GRASS (20G), CHOPPED FINELY

1 CUP (140G) ROASTED UNSALTED PEANUTS

1 Make coconut rice.

2 Meanwhile, make crisp coconut and peanut topping.

3 Heat half the oil in a wok over high heat; stir-fry beef, in batches, until browned. Remove from wok; cover to keep warm.

4 Heat remaining oil in a wok; stir-fry onion until soft. Add garlic, chilli, lemon grass, star anise, cinnamon, cardamom and beans; stir-fry for 3 mintues or until beans are almost tender. Return beef to wok with sauces; stir-fry until heated through. Remove from heat; stir in coriander.

5 Stir three-quarters of the topping mixture through the rice; scatter remaining topping over curry. Serve curry with rice.

COCONUT RICE Soak rice in cold water for 30 minutes. Drain; rinse until water runs clear. Place rice in a medium saucepan with coconut cream, turmeric and the water; bring to the boil, stirring occasionally. Reduce heat to low; simmer, covered, 15 minutes or until liquid is absorbed. Remove from heat; stand, covered, 5 minutes.

CRISP COCONUT & PEANUT TOPPING Preheat oven to 150°C/300°F. Heat oil in a wok over medium heat; stir-fry remaining ingredients, tossing continuously, for 15 minutes or until browned lightly. Transfer mixture to an oven tray; roast 20 minutes or until mixture has dried.

THE CRISP COCONUT AND PEANUT TOPPING, ALSO KNOWN AS SERUNDENG, IS USUALLY SPRINKLED OVER A HOT DISH JUST AS IT'S SERVED, MUCH LIKE A GREMOLATA, TO AWAKEN THE TASTEBUDS.

nutritional count per serving 56.7g total fat (29.9g saturated fat); 4222kJ (1008 cal); 68.4g carbohydrate; 51g protein; 10g fibre

NASI GORENG, WHICH TRANSLATES SIMPLY AS "FRIED RICE" IN INDONESIA AND MALAYSIA, WAS FIRST CREATED TO USE UP YESTERDAY'S LEFTOVERS. YOU NEED TO COOK 2 CUPS (400G) WHITE LONG-GRAIN RICE THE DAY BEFORE MAKING THIS RECIPE. SPREAD IT IN A THIN LAYER ON A TRAY AND REFRIGERATE IT OVERNIGHT.

NASI GORENG

1   Shell and devein prawns, leaving tails intact.

2   Heat half the oil in a wok over high heat; stir-fry sausage, in batches, until browned. Remove from wok.

3   Heat remaining oil in wok; stir-fry onion, capsicum, chilli, garlic, ginger and paste until vegetables soften. Add prawns and rice; stir-fry 2 minutes. Return sausage to wok with sauces and half the green onion; stir-fry until combined.

4   Heat extra oil in a large frying pan over medium heat; fry eggs, one side only, until just set.

5   Divide nasi goreng among plates, top each with an egg; sprinkle with remaining green onion.

TIP Dried chinese sausages, also called lap cheong, are usually made from pork and sold, in the Asian section of supermarkets or Asian grocers.

PREP + COOK TIME 40 MINUTES

SERVES 4

720G (1½ POUNDS) COOKED MEDIUM KING PRAWNS (SHRIMP)

1 TABLESPOON PEANUT OIL

175G (5½ OUNCES) DRIED CHINESE SAUSAGES, SLICED THICKLY

1 MEDIUM BROWN ONION (150G), SLICED THINLY

1 MEDIUM RED CAPSICUM (BELL PEPPER) (200G), SLICED THINLY

2 FRESH LONG RED CHILLIES, SLICED THINLY

2 CLOVES GARLIC, CRUSHED

2 TEASPOONS GRATED FRESH GINGER

1 TEASPOON SHRIMP PASTE

4 CUPS (600G) COLD COOKED WHITE LONG-GRAIN RICE

2 TABLESPOONS KECAP MANIS

1 TABLESPOON LIGHT SOY SAUCE

4 GREEN ONIONS (SCALLIONS), SLICED THINLY

1 TABLESPOON PEANUT OIL, EXTRA

4 EGGS

nutritional count per serving 25.7g total fat (7.4g saturated fat); 2730kJ (653 cal); 48.5g carbohydrate; 54.7g protein; 3.3g fibre

PORK & FENNEL RAGÙ WITH KUMARA GNOCCHI

PREP + COOK TIME 2 HOURS 50 MINUTES

SERVES 6

1.6KG (3¼-POUND) PIECE BONELESS PORK SHOULDER

2 TABLESPOONS PLAIN (ALL-PURPOSE) FLOUR

1 TABLESPOON EXTRA VIRGIN OLIVE OIL

2 MEDIUM LEEKS (700G), WHITE PART ONLY, SLICED

2 TRIMMED CELERY STALKS (200G), CHOPPED

2 MEDIUM FENNEL BULBS (600G), SLICED THINLY, FRONDS RESERVED

4 CLOVES GARLIC, CHOPPED

1 TEASPOON CHOPPED FRESH THYME LEAVES

¼ TEASPOON DRIED CHILLI FLAKES

2 CUPS (500ML) CHICKEN STOCK

2 CUPS (500ML) WATER

1 CUP (120G) GREEN SICILIAN OLIVES

1 TABLESPOON LEMON JUICE

KUMARA GNOCCHI

1KG (2 POUNDS) KUMARA (ORANGE SWEET POTATO), UNPEELED

120G (4 OUNCES) SOFT GOAT'S CHEESE, CRUMBLED

2 EGG YOLKS

1 CUP (150G) PLAIN (ALL-PURPOSE) FLOUR, APPROXIMATELY

1 Remove rind and trim fat from pork. Cut pork into six pieces, toss in flour; shake away excess. Heat oil in a casserole over high heat; cook pork, in batches, 10 minutes or until browned lightly. Remove from dish.

2 Cook leek, celery and sliced fennel in same dish stirring, over medium heat 8 minutes or until softened. Add garlic, thyme and chilli; cook, stirring, 1 minute or until fragrant. Add stock and the water; bring to the boil. Return pork to pan; stir to cover with liquid. Reduce heat to very low; simmer, covered, 2 hours or until tender, stirring occasionally.

3 Meanwhile, make kumara gnocchi.

4 Remove pork from pan; shred into smaller pieces. Return pork to pan with olives and juice. Season to taste. Cover; keep warm over low heat.

5 Cook gnocchi, in batches, in a large saucepan of boiling salted water 2 minutes or until gnocchi float to the surface. Remove gnocchi with a slotted spoon; drain on paper towel.

6 Serve gnocchi topped with ragù, sprinkled with reserved fennel fronds and extra thyme leaves, if you like.

KUMARA GNOCCHI Place whole kumara in a medium saucepan, cover with cold water. Cover pan with lid; bring to the boil. Reduce heat; simmer, partially covered, 45 minutes or until tender. Drain. Cool slightly; peel. Mash kumara in a large bowl until smooth. Cool to room temperature. Stir in cheese and egg yolks; season. Add enough of the flour to mix to a soft, slightly sticky dough. Divide dough into six portions; roll each portion on a floured surface into a 2cm (¾-inch) thick log. Using a floured knife, cut logs into 2cm (¾ inch) lengths. Place gnocchi on a large plastic-wrap-lined tray, in a single layer. Cover; refrigerate until required.

nutritional count per serving *12.7g total fat (4.8g saturated fat); 2499kJ (597 cal); 57.9g carbohydrate; 57.9g protein; 8.8g fibre*

PREPARE THE RAGÙ SEVERAL HOURS OR A DAY AHEAD;
REFRIGERATE UNTIL COLD THEN REMOVE ANY FAT
FROM THE SURFACE BEFORE REHEATING. YOU CAN USE
DRAINED PERSIAN FETTA INSTEAD OF GOAT'S CHEESE.

YOU CAN USE ALL GREEN ZUCCHINI OR A MIXTURE OF GREEN AND YELLOW.
THERE ARE TWO TYPES OF ZUCCHINI FLOWERS, MALE AND FEMALE. MALE
FLOWERS HAVE A STALK ATTACHED, WHILE FEMALE FLOWERS HAVE THE
'FRUIT', A SMALL ZUCCHINI ATTACHED, THE LATTER IS WHAT WE'VE USED.
IF ONLY THE FLOWERS ARE AVAILABLE, JUST ADD AN EXTRA ZUCCHINI TO
THE RECIPE TO COMPENSATE.

ZUCCHINI QUINOA SALAD WITH HALOUMI & CANDIED WALNUTS

1 Make candied walnuts, then white balsamic dressing.

2 Bring quinoa and the water to the boil in a medium saucepan; cook, covered, over low heat 15 minutes or until tender. Drain.

3 Meanwhile, combine zucchini, zucchini flowers, asparagus and 2 tablespoons of the oil in a large bowl; season. Cook zucchini mixture on a heated oiled barbecue (or chargrill plate or grill) for 5 minutes or until lightly charred and tender.

4 Brush haloumi with remaining oil; cook on cleaned, oiled barbecue for 1 minute each side or until browned. Tear roughly into pieces.

5 Place quinoa, zucchini mixture and haloumi in a large bowl with walnuts, herbs and dressing; toss gently to combine. Season to taste.

CANDIED WALNUTS Preheat oven to 200°C/400°F. Line an oven tray with baking paper. Whisk egg white in a medium bowl until foamy; stir in sugar, cayenne and salt, then nuts. Place nuts, in a single layer, on tray. Bake 8 minutes, stirring once, or until golden. Cool.

WHITE BALSAMIC DRESSING Whisk ingredients in a small bowl until combined. Season to taste.

TIP White balsamic vinegar is available from supermarkets. You can use white wine vinegar or lemon juice instead, if you prefer.

PREP + COOK TIME 45 MINUTES

SERVES 4

1 CUP (200G) QUINOA

3 CUPS (750ML) WATER

3 MEDIUM GREEN OR YELLOW ZUCCHINI (360G), SLICED THINLY

6 ZUCCHINI FLOWERS, ZUCCHINI ATTACHED (120G), HALVED LENGTHWAYS

170G (5½ OUNCES) ASPARAGUS

¼ CUP (60M) OLIVE OIL

180G (5½ OUNCES) HALOUMI, SLICED THINLY

1 CUP FRESH MINT LEAVES

¼ CUP CHOPPED FRESH CHIVES

CANDIED WALNUTS

1 EGG WHITE

2 TABLESPOONS CASTER SUGAR (SUPERFINE SUGAR)

½ TEASPOON CAYENNE PEPPER

½ TEASPOON SEA SALT FLAKES

1 CUP (100G) WALNUTS

WHITE BALSAMIC DRESSING

1 CLOVE GARLIC, CRUSHED

2 TABLESPOONS WHITE BALSAMIC VINEGAR

2 TABLESPOONS OLIVE OIL

2 TEASPOONS DIJON MUSTARD

1 TEASPOON CASTER SUGAR (SUPERFINE SUGAR)

nutritional count per serving *51.8g total fat (10g saturated fat); 3150kJ (752 cal); 45.6g carbohydrate; 23g protein; 7.9g fibre*

PIES WILL KEEP REFRIGERATED IN AN AIRTIGHT CONTAINER FOR UP TO 2 DAYS. THEY CAN BE FROZEN UNCOOKED OR COOKED. UNCOOKED PIES CAN BE BAKED FROM FROZEN. THAW COOKED PIES BEFORE REHEATING.

PEPPERED BEEF & MUSHROOM PIES

PREP + COOK TIME 1 HOUR 15 MINUTES (+ COOLING)

MAKES 8

3 SHEETS PUFF PASTRY

2 SHEETS SHORTCRUST PASTRY

1 TABLESPOON OLIVE OIL

300G (9½ OUNCES) BUTTON MUSHROOMS, CHOPPED COARSELY

1 MEDIUM BROWN ONION (150G), CHOPPED FINELY

600G (1¼ POUNDS) MINCED (GROUND) BEEF

2 TABLESPOONS CORNFLOUR (CORNSTARCH)

1½ CUPS (375ML) BEEF STOCK

2 TABLESPOONS TOMATO PASTE

2 TEASPOONS FRESHLY GROUND BLACK PEPPER

1 EGG, BEATEN LIGHTLY

1 Preheat oven to 200°C/400°F. Grease eight 9cm x 11.5cm (3¾-inch x 4¾-inch) oval pie tins.

2 Using an upturned pie tin as a guide, cut out eight ovals from puff pastry sheets. Refrigerate until needed.

3 Cut each sheet of shortcrust pastry into quarters to make eight squares. Roll squares out on a lightly floured surface until large enough to line each tin. Ease pastry into tins, press into bases and sides; trim edges. Prick bases with a fork. Line pastry with baking paper; fill with dried beans or rice. Place tins on oven trays. Bake 10 minutes. Remove beans and paper; bake further 5 minutes or until dry.

4 Heat half the oil in a large saucepan over high heat; cook mushrooms, stirring, for 8 minutes or until well browned. Remove from pan.

5 Heat remaining oil over medium-high heat in same pan; cook onion, stirring, until soft. Add beef; cook, stirring, over high heat until browned.

6 Blend cornflour and ¼ cup of the stock in a small bowl until smooth; stir in tomato paste. Return mushrooms to pan with cornflour mixture, remaining stock and pepper. Bring to the boil. Reduce heat; simmer, 3 minutes or until thickened. Cool.

7 Fill pastry cases with beef mixture. Brush edges of pastry with a little egg. Place puff pastry ovals on pies; press edges to seal. Brush tops with a little more egg. Cut a small slit in top of pies to allow steam to escape.

8 Bake pies for 30 minutes or until pastry is golden.

SERVING SUGGESTION Serve with tomato sauce (ketchup) or chutney.

nutritional count per pie *39.3g total fat (18.7g saturated fat); 2793kJ (667 cal); 49.3g carbohydrate; 28.3g protein; 2.5g fibre*

FOR THE BEST FLAVOUR, ENSURE THE MUSHROOMS ARE BROWNED WELL. USE A HEAVY-BASED FRYING PAN AND AVOID MOVING THEM AROUND TOO MUCH DURING COOKING — ALLOW THEM TO CATCH TO THE BASE OF THE PAN AND BROWN BEFORE TURNING. IF YOU DON'T HAVE A HEAVY-BASED PAN, HEAT THE PAN FIRST BEFORE ADDING THE OIL AND BUTTER.

FREE-FORM MUSHROOM & CHEESE TART

1 Preheat oven to 220°C/425°F. Line two oven trays with baking paper.

2 Heat half the butter and half the oil in a large heavy-based frying pan over high heat; cook half the mushrooms and half the shallots, stirring occasionally, 4 minutes or until golden. Season. Transfer to a medium bowl. Repeat with remaining butter, oil, mushrooms and shallots. Cool.

3 Meanwhile, process cream cheese and eggs until smooth; stir into mushroom mixture with parmesan and chopped parsley.

4 Place a pastry sheet on each oven tray. Spread mushroom mixture evenly between sheets, into a 16cm (6½-inch) round, leaving a 4cm (1½-inch) border. Brush border with a little of the extra egg. Fold in pastry corners, then remaining sides to partially cover filling and create a rim. Brush pastry rim with a little more egg. Scatter ricotta and thyme over filling.

5 Bake tarts 15 minutes or until pastry is puffed and golden. Serve tarts topped with parsley leaves.

TIP You can use garlic and herb cream cheese instead of the spring onion and chive flavour, or soft goat's cheese.

SERVING SUGGESTION Serve with a bitter green salad.

PREP + COOK TIME 1 HOUR (+ COOLING)

SERVES 4

60G (2 OUNCES) BUTTER

2 TABLESPOONS EXTRA VIRGIN OLIVE OIL

400G (12 OUNCES) SWISS BROWN MUSHROOMS, SLICED THINLY

400G (12 OUNCES) BUTTON MUSHROOMS, SLICED THINLY

2 SHALLOTS (50G), CHOPPED FINELY

200G (6½ OUNCES) SPRING ONION AND CHIVE CREAM CHEESE

2 EGGS

½ CUP (40G) FINELY GRATED PARMESAN

¼ CUP COARSELY CHOPPED FRESH FLAT-LEAF PARSLEY

2 SHEETS PUFF PASTRY

1 EGG, EXTRA, BEATEN LIGHTLY

100G (3 OUNCES) FRESH RICOTTA, CRUMBLED COARSELY

12 SMALL FRESH THYME SPRIGS

¼ CUP LOOSELY PACKED FRESH FLAT-LEAF PARSLEY LEAVES

nutritional count per serving *69.5g total fat (37.1g saturated fat); 3877kJ (926 cal); 45g carbohydrate; 27.9g protein; 6.5g fibre*

CHICKEN KOFTAS WITH FIG & SEED PILAF

PREP + COOK TIME 1 HOUR 20 MINUTES (+ REFRIGERATION)

SERVES 4

500G (1 POUND) MINCED (GROUND) CHICKEN

½ CUP (35G) STALE BREADCRUMBS

3 GREEN ONIONS (SCALLIONS), SLICED

2 CLOVES GARLIC, CRUSHED

1 TEASPOON GROUND CUMIN

¼ TEASPOON GROUND ALLSPICE

¼ TEASPOON GROUND CHILLI

2 TABLESPOONS OLIVE OIL

⅓ CUP FRESH CORIANDER (CILANTRO) SPRIGS

½ CUP (40G) FLAKED ALMONDS, ROASTED

FIG & SEED PILAF

2 TABLESPOONS OLIVE OIL

1 SMALL ONION (80G), CHOPPED FINELY

2 CLOVES GARLIC, CRUSHED

1 TABLESPOON FINELY GRATED ORANGE RIND

1 TEASPOON GROUND CINNAMON

½ TEASPOON GROUND CUMIN

500G (1 POUND) PACKAGED PRE-COOKED BROWN BASMATI RICE

1 CUP (250ML) CHICKEN STOCK

⅓ CUP (70G) CHOPPED DRIED FIGS

100G (3 OUNCES) BABY SPINACH LEAVES

2 TABLESPOONS PEPITAS (PUMPKIN SEEDS), TOASTED

2 TABLESPOONS SUNFLOWER SEEDS, TOASTED

1 Combine chicken, breadcrumbs, green onion, garlic and spices in a large bowl. Roll 2 tablespoons of mixture into long oval shapes; you should have 12. Place koftas on a baking-paper-lined oven tray; refrigerate 1 hour.

2 Make fig and seed pilaf.

3 Meanwhile, insert a skewer into each kofta; brush kofta well with oil. Cook kofta on heated chargrill plate (or barbecue or grill) on medium-high heat, turning occasionally, 8 minutes or until cooked through.

4 Serve kofta with pilaf, topped with coriander leaves and almonds.

FIG & SEED PILAF Heat oil in a large deep frying pan over medium-high heat; cook onion and garlic, for 3 minutes or until soft. Stir in rind and spices; cook for 2 minutes. Add rice; stir to coat. Add stock; bring to the boil. Reduce heat to medium; cook, covered, for 8 minutes. Remove from heat; stir in figs, spinach and seeds. Season to taste.

SERVING SUGGESTION Serve with labne or Greek-style yoghurt.

YOU WILL NEED TO SOAK 12 BAMBOO SKEWERS IN WATER FOR 30 MINUTES BEFORE YOU START THIS RECIPE.

nutritional count per serving *40.8g total fat (7.9g saturated fat); 3063kJ (732 cal); 51.6g carbohydrate; 36g protein; 8.4g fibre*

SLOW DESSERTS

THESE TARTS ARE PERFECT WHEN YOU'RE COOKING FOR A CROWD. AND WHEN YOU'RE NOT, JUST HALVE THE RECIPE TO MAKE A SINGLE TART. THIS RECIPE CAN BE MADE 3 HOURS AHEAD; STORE, COVERED AT ROOM TEMPERATURE UNTIL READY TO SERVE.

FIG & DATE TARTS

PREP + COOK TIME 1 HOUR 45 MINUTES (+ REFRIGERATION & FREEZING)

SERVES 16

3 CUPS (450G) PLAIN (ALL-PURPOSE) FLOUR

¼ CUP (40G) ICING SUGAR (CONFECTIONERS' SUGAR)

280G (9 OUNCES) BUTTER, CHOPPED

3 EGG YOLKS

2 TABLESPOONS MILK

8 FRESH FIGS (560G), QUARTERED

6 FRESH DATES (135G), QUARTERED

FILLING

2 EGGS

6 EGG YOLKS

¼ CUP (55G) CASTER SUGAR (SUPERFINE SUGAR)

1 TEASPOON VANILLA EXTRACT

600ML POURING CREAM

1 Sift flour and icing sugar into the bowl of a food processor with butter; process until mixture resembles breadcrumbs. Add egg yolks and milk; pulse until mixture almost comes together. Turn dough onto a floured surface, knead until smooth. Divide dough in half, shape into discs. Wrap discs in plastic wrap; refrigerate 30 minutes.

2 Roll out each disc on a lightly floured surface until large enough to line two 24cm (9½-inch) round loose-based tart pans. Lift pastry into each pan; ease into side, trim edges. Freeze 30 minutes.

3 Meanwhile, preheat oven to 190°C/375°F.

4 Place pastry cases on oven trays. Line pastry with baking paper, then fill with dried beans or rice. Bake 10 minutes. Remove paper and beans; bake a futher 10 minutes or until lightly browned and dry. Cool.

5 Meanwhile, make filling.

6 Divide figs and dates between pastry cases, top evenly with filling.

7 Bake tarts for 50 minutes, swapping trays from top to bottom or until custard is set. Serve tarts warm or cold.

FILLING Beat eggs, egg yolks, sugar and extract in a small bowl with electric mixer until thick and creamy; beat in cream until combined.

SERVING SUGGESTION Serve with thick (double) cream.

nutritional count per serving *32g total fat (16.2g saturated fat); 1905kJ (455 cal); 34g carbohydrate; 7.2g protein; 2.7g fibre*

CHOCOLATE HAZELNUT PUDDINGS WITH CRÈME ANGLAISE

1 Preheat oven to 180°C/350°F. Grease eight ¾ cup (180ml) metal dariole moulds.

2 Place chocolate and butter in a medium heatproof bowl over a medium saucepan of gently simmering water (don't let water touch base of bowl). Stir, occasionally, until melted and smooth. Remove from heat.

3 Beat eggs, egg yolks and sugar in a medium bowl with an electric mixer until thick and pale. Fold in sifted flour and ground hazelnuts; gently stir in chocolate mixture until just combined. Pour mixture into moulds; place on an oven tray.

4 Bake puddings 25 minutes or until a skewer inserted into the centre comes out with moist crumbs attached.

5 Meanwhile, make crème anglaise.

6 Carefully run a knife around edge of moulds, turn warm puddings onto plates. Dust with cocoa; drizzle with warm crème anglaise.

CRÈME ANGLAISE Bring milk and cream almost to the boil in a small saucepan. Whisk egg yolks, sugar and vanilla in a medium bowl until smooth; gradually whisk hot milk into egg yolk mixture. Return mixture to pan; stir with a wooden spoon over medium-low heat until custard thickens and coats the back of the spoon. Do not boil.

PREP + COOK TIME 1 HOUR 30 MINUTES

SERVES 8

200G (6½ OUNCES) DARK CHOCOLATE (70% COCOA), CHOPPED

200G (6½ OUNCES) UNSALTED BUTTER, CHOPPED COARSELY

4 EGGS

3 EGG YOLKS

1 CUP (220G) FIRMLY PACKED BROWN SUGAR

½ CUP (75G) PLAIN (ALL-PURPOSE) FLOUR

¾ CUP (125G) GROUND ROASTED HAZELNUTS

2 TEASPOONS DUTCH-PROCESSED COCOA

CRÈME ANGLAISE

1 CUP (250ML) MILK

½ CUP (125ML) POURING CREAM

6 EGG YOLKS

⅓ CUP (75G) CASTER SUGAR (SUPERFINE SUGAR)

1 TEASPOON VANILLA EXTRACT

nutritional count per serving *53g total fat (25.5g saturated fat); 3215kJ (768 cal); 62.3g carbohydrate; 13.3g protein; 2.2g fibre*

WHEN WHITE CHERRIES ARE AVAILABLE, USE A COMBINATION OF BOTH RED AND WHITE VARIETIES.

CHERRY SYRUP CAKE

PREP + COOK TIME 1 HOUR 30 MINUTES (+ COOLING)

SERVES 8

125G (4 OUNCES) UNSALTED BUTTER, SOFTENED

2 TEASPOONS FINELY GRATED LEMON RIND

¾ CUP (165G) CASTER SUGAR (SUPERFINE SUGAR)

2 EGGS

1¾ CUPS (260G) SELF-RAISING FLOUR

¾ CUP (180ML) BUTTERMILK

CHERRY SYRUP

1 CUP (220G) CASTER SUGAR (SUPERFINE SUGAR)

2 TABLESPOONS LEMON JUICE

1 LONG STRIP LEMON RIND

½ CUP (125ML) WATER

200G (6½ OUNCES) FRESH CHERRIES, STEMS ATTACHED

1 Preheat oven to 170°C/340°F. Grease a 8cm x 20cm (3¼-inch x 8-inch) loaf pan with a 1.25-litre (5-cup) capacity; line base and long sides with baking paper, extending the paper 5cm (2 inches) over sides.

2 Beat butter, rind and sugar in a small bowl with an electric mixer until light and fluffy. Beat in eggs, one at a time. Transfer mixture to a large bowl; stir in sifted flour and buttermilk, in two batches. Spread mixture into pan.

3 Bake cake 1 hour or until a skewer inserted into the centre comes out clean. Stand cake in pan 5 minutes before turning, top-side up, onto a wire rack placed over an oven tray; remove lining paper. Cool.

4 Meanwhile, make cherry syrup.

5 Slowly spoon hot syrup and cherries over cake. Place cake on a plate; pour syrup from tray into a small jug.

6 Serve cake slices, drizzled with remaining syrup.

CHERRY SYRUP Stir sugar, juice, rind and the water in a medium saucepan over heat, without boiling, until sugar dissolves. Bring to the boil; boil, without stirring, for 6 minutes. Add cherries; remove pan from heat. Cool.

nutritional count per serving *14.9g total fat (9.1g saturated fat); 1926kJ (460 cal); 76.3g carbohydrate; 6.4g protein; 1.6g fibre*

PEANUT BUTTER & JELLY BREAD & BUTTER PUDDING

1 Make peanut butter sauce.

2 Preheat oven to 180°C/350°F. Grease a 4-litre (16-cup) rectangle ovenproof dish.

3 Spread raspberry jam over half the bread slices, scatter with frozen raspberries; top with remaining bread to make a sandwich. Cut sandwich in half diagonally. Place sandwich halves upright in the dish, alternating between flat-side down and pointed-side down of each sandwich.

4 Combine milk, cream, sugar and extract in a medium saucepan; bring almost to the boil. Whisk eggs in a large bowl; whisking continuously, gradually add hot milk mixture to egg mixture. Gently pour milk mixture over the bread. Dot with butter; sprinkle with extra sugar.

5 Place ovenproof dish in a large roasting pan; add enough boiling water to come halfway up side of dish.

6 Bake pudding for 45 minutes or until just set. Remove pudding from roasting pan; stand 10 minutes. Serve pudding topped with fresh raspberries and drizzled with peanut butter sauce.

PEANUT BUTTER SAUCE Stir sugar and the water in a small saucepan over medium heat without boiling until sugar dissolves. Cook 10 minutes without stirring or until a golden caramel. Remove from heat. Taking care as the mixture will splutter, add cream. Return pan to heat; whisk until smooth. Whisk in peanut butter and peanuts. Cool.

TIPS Peanut butter sauce can be made up to 3 days ahead; store, covered, in an airtight container in the fridge. Leftover sauce can be used over ice-cream.

PREP + COOK TIME 1 HOUR 15 MINUTES

SERVES 8

¼ CUP (80G) RASPBERRY JAM

750G (1½-POUND) LOAF SLICED WHOLEMEAL BREAD

100G (3 OUNCES) FROZEN RASPBERRIES

2¼ CUPS (560ML) MILK

3 CUPS (750ML) POURING CREAM

⅓ CUP (75G) CASTER SUGAR (SUPERFINE SUGAR)

½ TEASPOON VANILLA EXTRACT

6 EGGS

10G (½ OUNCE) BUTTER

1 TABLESPOON CASTER SUGAR (SUPERFINE SUGAR), EXTRA

60G (2 OUNCES) FRESH RASPBERRIES

PEANUT BUTTER SAUCE

½ CUP (110G) CASTER SUGAR (SUPERFINE SUGAR)

2 TABLESPOONS WATER

1 CUP (250ML) THICKENED (HEAVY) CREAM

⅓ CUP (95G) SMOOTH PEANUT BUTTER

⅓ CUP (45G) COARSELY CHOPPED ROASTED PEANUTS

nutritional count per serving *85.7g total fat (46.7g saturated fat); 5689kJ (1359 cal); 177.6g carbohydrate; 30.2g protein; 7.2g fibre*

PUDDINGS

CHAI APRICOT BREAD & BUTTER PUDDINGS

PREP + COOK TIME 1 HOUR SERVES 4

Preheat oven to 200°C/400°F. Place 6 halved apricots, cut-side up, on a baking-paper-lined oven tray, brush with ¼ cup warmed ginger marmalade; roast 15 minutes. Reduce oven to 180°C/350°F. Combine ⅔ cup milk, 1 cup pouring cream, 2 tablespoons caster (superfine) sugar, 1 cinnamon stick, 1 star anise, 3 cloves and 1 bruised cardamom pod in a medium saucepan; bring to the boil. Remove from heat; stand 20 minutes. Cut a small baguette into 24 thin slices. Spread slices with ¼ cup ginger marmalade, sandwich with half an apricot. Stand 3 sandwiches upright in each of four 1¼-cup ramekins. Return milk mixture to the boil. Whisk 2 eggs in a bowl; gradually whisk in hot milk mixture. Strain milk mixture into ramekins; sprinkle with 1 tablespoon caster (superfine) sugar. Place ramekins in a baking dish; add enough boiling water to dish to come halfway up side of ramekins. Bake 20 minutes or until just set. Remove puddings from water; stand 10 minutes. Top with 4 small fresh apricots cut into thirds. Serve with thick (double) cream.

FIG & EARL GREY TEA BREAD & BUTTER PUDDING

PREP + COOK TIME 1 HOUR 15 MINUTES SERVES 6

Preheat oven to 180°C/350°F. Combine 2¼ cups milk, 3 cups pouring cream and 2 tablespoons earl grey tea leaves in a medium saucepan; bring to the boil. Remove from heat; stand 10 minutes. Meanwhile, melt 30g (1 ounce) butter in a small frying pan over high heat; cook 6 halved figs with 2 tablespoons brown sugar, turning, for 2 minutes or until caramelised. Remove from heat. Stir ⅓ cup caster (superfine) sugar and ½ teaspoon vanilla extract into milk mixture; return to the boil. Whisk 6 eggs in a bowl; whisking continuously, gradually add hot milk mixture. Cut 450g (14½ ounces) brioche loaf into 1.5cm (¾-inch) thick slices. Layer brioche and figs in a 2-litre (8-cup) ovenproof dish. Strain milk mixture over brioche; press brioche gently into mixture. Stand 5 minutes. Dot with 10g (⅓ ounce) butter, sprinkle with 1 tablespoon caster sugar. Place dish in a roasting pan; add enough boiling water to come halfway up side of dish. Bake 30 minutes or until just set. Remove pudding from water; stand 10 minutes. Serve topped with 2 medium fresh figs torn in half, drizzled with 1 tablespoon honey.

APPLE STREUSEL BREAD & BUTTER PUDDING

PREP + COOK TIME 1 HOUR 15 MINUTES SERVES 6

Preheat oven to 180°C/350°F. Combine ⅓ cup plain (all-purpose) flour, 2 tablespoons self-raising flour, ¼ cup firmly packed brown sugar and ½ teaspoon mixed spice in a bowl; rub in 80g (2½ ounces) chopped butter until mixture resembles breadcrumbs. Cover; freeze 1 hour or until firm. Meanwhile, peel, core and thickly slice 5 medium (750g) granny smith apples; place in a saucepan with ¼ cup water. Bring to the boil. Reduce heat; simmer, covered, 5 minutes or until softened. Drain well; stir in 2 tablespoons caster (superfine) sugar, ½ teaspoon finely grated lemon rind and ¼ teaspoon ground cinnamon. Slice a 420g (13½-ounce) ciabatta loaf into 1.5cm (¾-inch) thick slices, place staggered in a 3-litre (12-cup) ovenproof dish. Divide apple mixture between bread. Combine 1½ cups milk, 2 cups pouring cream, ⅓ cup caster (superfine) sugar and ½ teaspoon vanilla extract in a medium saucepan; bring to the boil. Whisk 4 eggs in a large bowl; gradually whisk hot milk mixture into egg mixture. Gently pour milk mixture over the bread. Sprinkle top with crumble mixture. Place dish in a roasting pan; add enough boiling water to come halfway up side of dish. Bake 40 minutes or until just set. Remove pudding from water; stand 10 minutes. Dust with 1 teaspoon of icing (confectioners') sugar. Serve with vanilla ice-cream or cold custard.

CHOCOLATE & IRISH CREAM CROISSANT PUDDING

PREP + COOK TIME 50 MINUTES SERVES 6

Preheat oven to 170°C/340°F. Cut 8 croissants (400g) in half lengthways, sprinkle 100g (3 ounces) coarsely chopped dark chocolate on cut sides; sandwich together. Arrange croissants in a 1.75-litre (7-cup) oval ovenproof dish. Combine 1 cup milk, 2 cups pouring cream, ⅓ cup caster (superfine) sugar and ½ teaspoon vanilla extract in a medium saucepan; bring to the boil. Whisk 4 eggs in a large bowl; gradually whisk in hot milk mixture, then stir in ¾ cup irish cream whisky. Pour milk mixture over croissants; top with 80g (2½ ounces) coarsely chopped dark chocolate and 1 tablespoon caster (superfine) sugar. Place dish in a roasting pan; add enough boiling water to come halfway up side of dish. Bake 35 minutes or until just set. Remove pudding from water; stand 10 minutes. Serve dusted with 1 teaspoon of icing (confectioners') sugar.

CARAMEL & PEANUT BUTTER MOUSSE MERINGUE CAKE

PREP + COOK TIME 1 HOUR 40 MINUTES (+ COOLING & REFRIGERATION)

SERVES 8

3 EGG WHITES

1 CUP (160G) ICING SUGAR (CONFECTIONERS' SUGAR)

3 TEASPOONS CORNFLOUR (CORNSTARCH)

¾ CUP (100G) GROUND ALMONDS

4 TEASPOONS POWDERED GELATINE

2 TABLESPOONS COLD WATER

½ CUP (140G) SMOOTH PEANUT BUTTER

½ CUP (170G) CANNED CARAMEL TOP 'N' FILL

1 CUP (250ML) THICKENED (HEAVY) CREAM

1½ CUPS (375ML) THICK (DOUBLE) CREAM

1 TABLESPOON DUTCH-PROCESSED COCOA

PEANUT CARAMEL SAUCE

½ CUP (110G) CASTER SUGAR (SUPERFINE SUGAR)

2 TABLESPOONS WATER

1 CUP (250ML) THICKENED (HEAVY) CREAM

⅓ CUP (70G) SMOOTH PEANUT BUTTER

⅓ CUP (45G) COARSELY CHOPPED ROASTED PEANUTS

1 Preheat oven to 160°C/325°F. Lock the base in two 22cm (9-inch) springform pans upside down; grease, then line the base and side with baking paper.

2 Beat egg whites in a small bowl with an electric mixer until soft peaks form. Gradually add sifted icing sugar, beating until thick and glossy. Beat in cornflour and ground almonds until well combined. Divide mixture between pans; smooth surface with a palette knife.

3 Bake meringues for 40 minutes, swapping pans from top to bottom halfway through cooking time, or until crisp and dry. Cool in oven with door ajar.

4 Meanwhile, make peanut caramel sauce.

5 To make mousse, sprinkle gelatine over the water in a small bowl; stand for 5 minutes. Whisk peanut butter, caramel top 'n' fill and thickened cream in a small saucepan over low heat until well combined. Increase heat to medium; bring to the boil. Remove from heat; stir in gelatine mixture until dissolved. Transfer to a medium bowl; cool. Whisk thick cream just until soft peaks form; fold into peanut butter mixture.

6 Spoon mousse on one meringue in pan. Remove second meringue from pan; place on top of mousse. Refrigerate for 2 hours or until set.

7 Before serving, dust cake with cocoa. Serve topped with peanut caramel sauce.

PEANUT CARAMEL SAUCE Stir sugar and the water in a small saucepan over medium heat, without boiling, until sugar dissolves. Cook 10 minutes without stirring or until mixture becomes a golden brown caramel. Remove pan from heat; carefully add cream, as the mixture will splutter. Return pan to heat; stir until smooth, then stir in peanut butter and peanuts. Cool.

TIP The meringue layers can be made up to 3 days ahead; store in an airtight container at room temperature.

nutritional count per serving *77g total fat (38g saturated fat); 4043kJ (966 cal); 52.7g carbohydrate; 18g protein; 4.3g fibre*

VIETNAM'S FRENCH INFLUENCES ARE OBVIOUS IN THIS DISH. COMMON THROUGHOUT THE COUNTRY, IT IS CALLED BÁNH CARAMEL, CARAMEN OR KEM CARAMEL IN NORTHERN VIETNAM OR BÁNH FLAN OR KEM FLAN IN SOUTHERN VIETNAM.

VIETNAMESE COFFEE CRÈME CARAMEL

1 Preheat oven to 160°C/325°F.

2 Stir sugar and the water in a small saucepan over medium-low heat without boiling until sugar dissolves. Bring to the boil. Boil, without stirring, for 5 minutes, brushing down the side of the pan occasionally with a wet pastry brush to remove any undissolved sugar crystals, or until mixture turns a golden caramel. Immediately pour into a 20cm (8-inch) round cake pan; cool.

3 Meanwhile, stir coffee granules and extra boiling water in a small cup until coffee dissolves; cool. Place coffee mixture in a large bowl; whisk in egg yolks, then sweetened condensed milk and milk until smooth.

4 Pour milk mixture over caramel in cake pan. Place cake pan in a roasting pan; add enough boiling water to come one-third of the way up side of the cake pan.

5 Bake 45 minutes or until mixture is just set. Remove cake pan from water; cool to room temperature. Cover; refrigerate overnight.

6 Carefully run a knife around the inside of the pan to loosen custard from the side of the pan, then turn onto a plate with a rim. Serve topped with coconut and nuts.

YOU WILL NEED TO MAKE THIS RECIPE A DAY AHEAD.

PREP + COOK TIME 1 HOUR (+ REFRIGERATION)

SERVES 6

¾ CUP (165G) CASTER SUGAR (SUPERFINE SUGAR)

⅓ CUP (80ML) BOILING WATER

3 TEASPOONS INSTANT ESPRESSO COFFEE GRANULES

2 TABLESPOONS BOILING WATER, EXTRA

6 EGG YOLKS

395G (12½ OUNCES) CANNED SWEETENED CONDENSED MILK

1½ CUPS (375ML) MILK

2 TABLESPOONS MOIST COCONUT FLAKES, TOASTED

¼ CUP (40G) ROASTED CASHEWS

nutritional count per serving *18.4g total fat (8.9g saturated fat); 1998kJ (477 cal); 68.9g carbohydrate; 12g protein; 0.7g fibre*

COCONUT & PASSIONFRUIT TART

YOU WILL NEED TO MAKE THIS TART A DAY AHEAD.

PREP + COOK TIME 1 HOUR 30 MINUTES (+ REFRIGERATION, FREEZING & COOLING)

SERVES 8

1⅔ CUPS (250G) PLAIN (ALL-PURPOSE) FLOUR

¼ CUP (40G) ICING SUGAR (CONFECTIONERS' SUGAR)

¼ TEASPOON SALT

150G (4½ OUNCES) COLD UNSALTED BUTTER, CHOPPED

1 EGG

1 EGG YOLK

FILLING

2 EGGS

1 CUP (220G) CASTER SUGAR (SUPERFINE SUGAR)

½ CUP (125ML) STRAINED PASSIONFRUIT JUICE

1 TEASPOON GRATED ORANGE RIND

1½ CUPS (375ML) POURING CREAM

3 CUPS (240G) DESICCATED COCONUT

1 Process flour, icing sugar, a pinch of salt and butter until mixture resembles fine breadcrumbs, add egg and yolk; process until mixture just comes together. Form dough into a disc, wrap in plastic wrap; refrigerate 30 minutes.

2 Roll out dough on a lightly floured surface until 3mm (⅛-inch) thick and large enough to line a 28cm (11¼-inch) round loose-based tart pan with pastry. Cover; freeze 1 hour.

3 Preheat oven to 200°C/400°F.

4 Line pastry case with baking paper; fill with dried beans or rice. Bake 10 minutes. Remove paper and beans; bake a further 10 minutes or until pastry is golden and dry. Cool. Reduce oven to 180°C/350°F.

5 Meanwhile, make filling.

6 Spoon filling into pastry case. Bake 35 minutes or until just set and lightly browned. Cool. Refrigerate overnight before serving.

FILLING Beat eggs and sugar in a small bowl with an electric mixer until pale and smooth. Beat in juice and rind until just combined, then cream and coconut until just combined.

SERVING SUGGESTION Serve topped wtih extra passionfruit and thick (double) cream.

FOR STRAINED PASSIONFRUIT JUICE, PROCESS THE PULP OF 8 PASSIONFRUIT FOR A FEW SECONDS TO LOOSEN THE JUICE AWAY FROM THE SEEDS. PUSH THROUGH A FINE SIEVE, PRESSING DOWN FIRMLY ON SOLIDS. DISCARD SEEDS.

nutritional count per serving *54.7g total fat (37.4g saturated fat); 3258kJ (774 cal); 59g carbohydrate; 9.8g protein; 8g fibre*

FROZEN CHOCOLATE MOUSSE CAKE

1   Grease a 14cm x 21cm (5½-inch x 8½-inch) loaf pan; line base and two long sides with baking paper, extending the paper 5cm (2-inches) above edges of pan.

2   Place chocolate in a small heatproof bowl over a small saucepan of gently simmering water (don't allow bowl to touch water); stir until melted.

3   Process ricotta and sugar until smooth; transfer to a medium bowl. Stir in melted chocolate and nougat.

4   Beat cream in a small bowl with an electric mixer until soft peaks form. Fold cream into chocolate mixture. Spoon mixture into pan, cover with foil; freeze overnight.

5   Just before serving, make chocolate sauce.

6   Turn mousse cake onto a serving platter; drizzle with a little of the chocolate sauce. Scatter with raspberries and nuts. Serve sliced with remaining chocolate sauce.

CHOCOLATE SAUCE Bring cream almost to the boil in a small saucepan over low-medium heat. Add chocolate; stir until smooth.

PREP + COOK TIME 40 MINUTES (+ FREEZING)

SERVES 8

200G (6½ OUNCES) DARK (SEMI-SWEET) CHOCOLATE, CHOPPED

2¼ CUPS (450G) RICOTTA

½ CUP (110G) CASTER SUGAR (SUPERFINE SUGAR)

150G (4½ OUNCES) ALMOND NOUGAT, CHOPPED COARSELY

300ML THICKENED (HEAVY) CREAM

125G (4 OUNCES) RASPBERRIES

¼ CUP (20G) FLAKED ALMONDS, ROASTED

CHOCOLATE SAUCE

½ CUP (125ML) POURING CREAM

200G (6½ OUNCES) MILK CHOCOLATE (33% COCOA), CHOPPED FINELY

THE CHOCOLATE SAUCE WILL TASTE MUCH MORE CHOCOLATEY, RATHER THAN SUGARY, IF YOU BUY MILK CHOCOLATE WITH A HIGH PERCENTAGE OF COCOA SOLIDS IN IT. LOOK IN THE CONFECTIONERY AISLE FOR A GOOD QUALITY ONE.

nutritional count per serving *42.9g total fat (24.6g saturated fat); 2825kJ (675 cal); 63g carbohydrate; 11.4g protein; 1.4g fibre*

WHEN YOU'RE NOT USING THE PASTRY, KEEP IT COVERED WITH A DAMP TEA TOWEL TO PREVENT THE PASTRY FROM DRYING OUT.

CHOCOLATE BAKLAVA

PREP + COOK TIME 1 HOUR (+ COOLING & STANDING)

MAKES 12

6 SHEETS FILLO PASTRY

60G (2 OUNCES) BUTTER, MELTED

FILLING

¾ CUP (100G) PISTACHIOS

1 CUP (100G) WALNUTS

100G (3 OUNCES) DARK (SEMI-SWEET) CHOCOLATE, CHOPPED COARSELY

2 TABLESPOONS CASTER SUGAR (SUPERFINE SUGAR)

1 TEASPOON GROUND CINNAMON

1 TABLESPOON FINELY GRATED ORANGE RIND

HONEY SYRUP

¾ CUP (165G) CASTER SUGAR (SUPERFINE SUGAR)

¾ CUP (180ML) WATER

¼ CUP (90G) HONEY

2 TABLESPOONS ORANGE JUICE

1 ORANGE (260G), RIND CUT INTO LONG THIN STRIPS

1 Preheat oven to 190°C/375°F. Line a large oven tray with baking paper.

2 Make filling.

3 Layer three pastry sheets, brushing each with a little of the butter. Spread half the filling over pastry, leaving a 3cm (1¼-inch) border along both long sides. Starting at one long side, roll up pastry to form a log; cut in half. Place on oven tray; brush with butter. Repeat with remaining pastry, butter and filling.

4 Bake baklava 20 minutes or until golden and crisp.

5 Meanwhile, make honey syrup.

6 Stand baklava on tray 5 minutes to cool slightly, then transfer to a shallow heatproof dish, just large enough to hold it. Pour hot syrup over baklava; stand 3 hours or until syrup is absorbed. To serve, cut each log on the diagonal into three pieces.

FILLING Place nuts on an oven tray; roast in oven 5 minutes or until browned lightly. Cool completely. Process nuts with remaining ingredients until finely chopped.

HONEY SYRUP Stir sugar, the water and honey in a small saucepan, over medium heat, without boiling, until sugar dissolves. Simmer for 10 minutes or until thickened slightly. Stir in juice and rind.

nutritional count per piece *16.6g total fat (4.9g saturated fat); 1239kJ (296 cal); 33.5g carbohydrate; 4g protein; 1.8g fibre*

LEMON CURD CAKE

1 Make lemon curd, then lemon syrup.

2 Preheat oven to 180°C/350°F. Grease two deep 22cm (9-inch) round cake pans; line bases and sides with baking paper.

3 Beat butter and sugar in a large bowl with an electric mixer until light and fluffy. Beat in eggs, one at a time until combined. Stir in sifted flours, crème fraîche and juice, in two batches. Divide mixture between pans; smooth surface.

4 Bake cakes 35 minutes or until a skewer inserted into the centre comes out clean. Stand cakes in pans 5 minutes before turning, top-side up, onto wire racks to cool.

5 Using a serrated knife, trim tops of cakes so they are level. Split each cake into two layers. Place one layer on a plate; brush with a little of the syrup and spread with half the curd. Repeat layering with remaining cake layers, syrup and curd, finishing with a cake layer.

6 Make fluffy frosting; spread over top and sides of cake.

LEMON CURD Whisk eggs, egg yolks and sugar in a medium saucepan until smooth. Chop butter into small cubes; add butter, rind and juice to pan. Whisk over low heat until curd thickens. Strain into a medium bowl. Cover surface with plastic wrap; cool.

LEMON SYRUP Stir sugar and the water in a small saucepan over medium heat, without boiling, until sugar dissolves. Bring to the boil; boil without stirring 3 minutes or until syrup is thickened. Remove from heat; stir in liqueur. Cool.

FLUFFY FROSTING Stir sugar and the water in a small saucepan over high heat without boiling until sugar dissolves. Bring to the boil; boil without stirring, 5 minutes. Remove from heat; allow bubbles to subside. Immediately, beat egg whites in a small bowl with an electric mixer until stiff peaks form; with mixer operating on medium speed, gradually pour in syrup. Continue beating 10 minutes or until frosting is stiff and barely warm.

PREP + COOK TIME 2 HOURS (+ COOLING)

SERVES 12

250G (8 OUNCES) BUTTER, SOFTENED

2 CUPS (440G) CASTER SUGAR (SUPERFINE SUGAR)

4 EGGS

2 CUPS (300G) SELF-RAISING FLOUR

1 CUP (150G) PLAIN (ALL-PURPOSE) FLOUR

200G (6½ OUNCES) CRÈME FRAÎCHE

2 TABLESPOONS LEMON JUICE

LEMON CURD

4 EGGS

4 EGG YOLKS

1½ CUPS (330G) CASTER SUGAR (SUPERFINE SUGAR)

150G (4½ OUNCES) COLD BUTTER

2 TABLESPOONS FINELY GRATED LEMON RIND

⅔ CUP (160ML) LEMON JUICE

LEMON SYRUP

⅓ CUP (75G) CASTER SUGAR (SUPERFINE SUGAR)

⅓ CUP (80ML) WATER

2 TABLESPOONS LIMONCELLO LIQUEUR

FLUFFY FROSTING

1 CUP (220G) CASTER SUGAR (SUPERFINE SUGAR)

⅓ CUP (80ML) WATER

2 EGG WHITES

nutritional count per serving *38.9g total fat (23.4g saturated fat); 3590kJ (858 cal); 119g carbohydrate; 11 g protein; 1.5g fibre*

ROSEWATER & PISTACHIO CHEESECAKE CUPS

PREP + COOK TIME 55 MINUTES (+ COOLING)

SERVES 16

100G (3 OUNCES) PISTACHIOS

½ CUP (110G) CASTER SUGAR (SUPERFINE SUGAR)

½ TEASPOON GROUND CINNAMON

½ TEASPOON GROUND CARDAMOM

6 SHEETS FILLO PASTRY, HALVED CROSSWAYS

50G (1½ OUNCES) BUTTER, MELTED

750G (1½ POUNDS) CREAM CHEESE, SOFTENED

2¼ CUPS (360G) ICING SUGAR (CONFECTIONERS' SUGAR)

2 TABLESPOONS ROSEWATER

1½ TEASPOONS LEMON RIND

¼ CUP (60ML) LEMON JUICE

¾ CUP (180G) POMEGRANATE SEEDS

100G (3 OUNCES) ROSE-FLAVOURED PERSIAN FAIRY FLOSS

1 Preheat oven to 180°C/350°F. Line two oven trays with baking paper.

2 Place nuts on one oven tray; roast for 5 minutes or until browned lightly. Transfer to a food processor; cool. Process cooled nuts until ground finely. Place ground nuts in a small bowl with caster sugar and spices; stir to combine. Wash oven tray to cool; line with baking paper.

3 Place one pastry half on each oven tray; lightly brush with melted butter, sprinkle ¼ cup nut spice mixture between the two pastry halves. Repeat layering with pastry halves, butter and nut mixture. Top with remaining pastry halves; brush with the remaining butter and sprinkle with remaining nut mixture. Bake 15 minutes or until pastry is golden; cool. Crumble pastry into rough pieces; store in an airtight container until needed.

4 Beat cream cheese, sifted icing sugar, rosewater, rind and juice in a small bowl with electric mixer until soft peaks form.

5 Spoon ¼-cups of cream cheese mixture into ¾-cup (180ml) glasses; sprinkle with crumbled pastry and pomegranate seeds. Just before serving, top with fairy floss.

PERSIAN FAIRY FLOSS, ALSO CALLED PASHMAK, IS AVAILABLE FROM DELIS AND SPECIALIST FOOD SHOPS.

nutritional count per ¾-cup serving   *13.6g total fat (6.7g saturated fat); 1243kJ (297 cal); 40.9g carbohydrate; 4g protein; 0.5g fibre*

YOU CAN SERVE THE CHEESECAKE CUPS AS PART OF A
DESSERT BUFFET. FOR A MAIN DESSERT, ASSEMBLE THE
RECIPE IN 1½-CUP (375ML) GLASSES. CHEESECAKE CUPS
CAN BE ASSEMBLED SEVERAL HOURS AHEAD WITHOUT
THE FAIRY FLOSS; STORE, COVERED, IN THE FRIDGE.

SPICED SPONGE & RHUBARB ROULADE

1 Preheat oven to 200°C/400°F. Grease a 26cm x 32cm (10½-inch x 12¾-inch) swiss roll pan; line base with baking paper, extending the paper 5cm (2 inches) over the long sides.

2 Beat egg yolks and sugar in a medium bowl with an electric mixer 5 minutes or until very thick. Pour the hot water down inside of the bowl, add chocolate; gently fold in combined sifted flour and spices until just combined. Transfer to a medium bowl.

3 Beat egg whites in a medium bowl with an electric mixer until soft peaks form. Fold egg whites into chocolate mixture, in two batches, until just combined. Spread mixture into pan.

4 Bake cake 12 minutes or until golden and sponge springs back when pressed lightly with a finger.

5 Meanwhile, place a piece of baking paper, cut just larger than the pan, on a work surface; sprinkle evenly with extra sugar. Turn hot sponge onto sugar-covered-paper, peel away lining paper; trim crisped edges with a sharp knife. Working quickly, and using paper as a guide, roll sponge up from a long side. Cool for 5 minutes. Unroll sponge, remove paper; reroll, cover with a clean tea towel. Cool.

6 Meanwhile, make roasted rhubarb. Make mascarpone cream.

7 Unroll sponge; spread with mascarpone cream, leaving a 2.5cm (1-inch) border. Top with rhubarb. Reroll sponge to enclose filling. Serve roulade drizzled with rhubarb pan juices.

ROASTED RHUBARB Combine ingredients in a medium bowl; transfer to a small shallow baking dish. Roast in oven for 10 minutes, stirring halfway, or until rhubarb is tender.

MASCARPONE CREAM Beat cream and mascarpone in a small bowl with an electric mixer until soft peaks form.

TIP This recipe is best made on day of serving.

PREP + COOK TIME 45 MINUTES (+ COOLING)

SERVES 10

5 EGGS, SEPARATED

⅔ CUP (150G) CASTER SUGAR (SUPERFINE SUGAR)

1½ TABLESPOONS HOT WATER

80G (2½ OUNCES) WHITE CHOCOLATE, GRATED FINELY

⅔ CUP (100G) SELF-RAISING FLOUR

1 TEASPOON GROUND CINNAMON

½ TEASPOON GROUND NUTMEG

¼ TEASPOON GROUND CLOVES

¼ TEASPOON GROUND CARDAMOM

¼ CUP (55G) CASTER SUGAR (SUPERFINE SUGAR), EXTRA

ROASTED RHUBARB

500G (1 POUND) RHUBARB, TRIMMED, CUT INTO 5CM (2-INCH) LENGTHS

⅓ CUP (75G) FIRMLY PACKED BROWN SUGAR

2 TEASPOONS FINELY GRATED ORANGE RIND

1 TABLESPOON ORANGE JUICE

2.5CM (1-INCH) PIECE FRESH GINGER (12.5G), GRATED

MASCARPONE CREAM

½ CUP (125ML) THICKENED (HEAVY) CREAM

1 CUP (250G) MASCARPONE

nutritional count per serving *20.4g total fat (12.8g saturated fat); 1576kJ (376 cal); 41.7g carbohydrate; 7.1g protein; 1.8g fibre*

THE CAKE CAN BE MADE A DAY AHEAD; STORE IN AN AIRTIGHT CONTAINER AT ROOM TEMPERATURE. THE HAZELNUT CREAM IS BEST MADE ON THE DAY OF SERVING.

FLOURLESS CHOCOLATE, PRUNE & HAZELNUT CAKE

PREP + COOK TIME 1 HOUR 15 MINUTES (+ STANDING)

SERVES 10

1 CUP (170G) PITTED PRUNES, CHOPPED FINELY

½ CUP (125ML) HAZELNUT-FLAVOURED LIQUEUR

200G (6½ OUNCES) DARK (SEMI-SWEET) CHOCOLATE, CHOPPED COARSELY

125G (4 OUNCES) BUTTER, SOFTENED

5 EGGS, SEPARATED

⅔ CUP (150G) FIRMLY PACKED BROWN SUGAR

1¼ CUPS (180G) GROUND HAZELNUTS

2 TEASPOONS DUTCH-PROCESSED COCOA

HAZELNUT CREAM

300ML POURING CREAM

2 TABLESPOONS ICING SUGAR (CONFECTIONERS') SUGAR

2 TABLESPOONS HAZELNUT-FLAVOURED LIQUEUR

1 Place prunes and liqueur in a small saucepan; bring to the boil. Reduce heat; simmer, uncovered, for 2 minutes or until liqueur is reduced by half. Remove from heat; cool.

2 Meanwhile, preheat oven to 180°C/350°F. Grease a deep 22cm (9-inch) round cake pan; line base and side with baking paper.

3 Stir chocolate and butter in a small saucepan over low heat until melted and smooth. Cool to room temperature.

4 Beat egg yolks and sugar in a small bowl with an electric mixer until thick and creamy. Transfer mixture to a large bowl; fold in prune mixture, chocolate mixture and ground hazelnuts.

5 Beat egg whites in a small bowl with an electric mixer until soft peaks form; fold into chocolate mixture, in two batches. Pour mixture into pan.

6 Bake cake for 50 minutes or until a skewer inserted into the centre comes out with moist crumbs attached. Stand cake in pan for 15 minutes; turn cake, top-side up, onto a wire rack to cool.

7 Make hazelnut cream.

8 Dust cake with cocoa; serve with hazelnut cream.

HAZELNUT CREAM Beat cream and sugar in a small bowl with an electric mixer until firm peaks form. Stir in liqueur.

nutritional count per serving *40g total fat (18.3g saturated fat); 2438kJ (582 cal); 43.6g carbohydrate; 8.4g protein; 2.1g fibre*

HONEY SAFFRON SYRUP CAKES

1   Combine saffron and juice in a small bowl; stand 20 minutes.

2   Meanwhile, preheat oven to 180°C/350°F. Grease 12 oval friand pans; line bases with baking paper.

3   Beat butter, sugar, rind and 1 teaspoon of the vanilla paste in a small bowl with an electric mixer for 3 minutes or until pale and fluffy. Beat in egg yolks, one at a time, until combined. Transfer mixture to a large bowl. Stir in flour and yoghurt, in two batches; stir in saffron mixture.

4   Beat egg whites in a small bowl with an electric mixer until soft peaks form. Stir into cake mixture, in two batches. Spoon ⅓ cup mixture into each pan hole.

5   Bake cakes 25 minutes or until a skewer inserted into the centre comes out clean.

6   Meanwhile, make honey saffron syrup.

7   Turn hot cakes, top-side up, onto a wire rack over an oven tray. Brush hot syrup over hot cakes.

8   Combine crème fraîche, honey and remaining vanilla bean paste in a small bowl. Serve cakes topped with crème fraîche mixture and nuts; drizzle with remaining syrup.

HONEY SAFFRON SYRUP Stir ingredients in a small saucepan over medium heat until sugar dissolves. Bring to the boil. Remove from heat; stand 5 minutes. Discard whole spices.

TIP The cakes can be made a day ahead. Store in an airtight container at room temperature.

PREP + COOK TIME 1 HOUR 15 MINUTES (+ REFRIGERATION & STANDING)

MAKES 12

¼ TEASPOON SAFFRON THREADS

2 TEASPOONS LEMON JUICE

200G (6½ OUNCES) UNSALTED BUTTER, SOFTENED, CHOPPED

¾ CUP (165G) CASTER SUGAR (SUPERFINE SUGAR)

2 TEASPOONS FINELY GRATED LEMON RIND

2 TEASPOONS VANILLA BEAN PASTE

3 EGGS, SEPARATED

1⅔ CUPS (250G) SELF-RAISING FLOUR

1 CUP (280G) GREEK-STYLE YOGHURT

1 CUP (240G) CRÈME FRAÎCHE

2 TABLESPOONS HONEY

½ CUP (55G) ROASTED NATURAL ALMONDS, CHOPPED COARSELY

HONEY SAFFRON SYRUP

¼ TEASPOON SAFFRON THREADS

½ TEASPOON VANILLA BEAN PASTE

¾ CUP (180ML) WATER

¼ CUP (90G) HONEY

¾ CUP (165G) CASTER SUGAR (SUPERFINE SUGAR)

2 STRIPS LEMON RIND

⅓ CUP (80ML) LEMON JUICE

6 CLOVES

2 CINNAMON STICKS

nutritional count per cake *25.6g total fat (14.9g saturated fat); 2022kJ (483 cal); 59.7g carbohydrate; 4.9g protein; 1.2g fibre*

FLAVOURS OF THE EAST MENU FOR 4

The flavours of this easy casual menu are flexible enough to suit winter or summer entertaining. Swap coriander for parsley and fetta for parmesan in the salad if you like. The baklava is even more luscious served with bought fig or caramel ice-cream.

STARTER

WARM BEEF & HUMMUS SALAD (PAGE 19)

MAIN

SPICY FISH TAGINE WITH RED COUSCOUS (PAGE 15)

SIDE

KOHLRABI, CABBAGE & PARMESAN SALAD (PAGE 86)

DESSERT

CHOCOLATE BAKLAVA (PAGE 126)

WARM BEEF & HUMMUS SALAD (PAGE 19)

SEAFOOD BISQUE (PAGE 61)

COMFORT FOOD DINNER FOR 8

The osso buco (without the risotto) and the crème anglaise can be made a day ahead. For a less hearty menu omit the starter, or for a lunch serve the bisque rather than the osso buco.

STARTER

SEAFOOD BISQUE (PAGE 61)

MAIN

OSSO BUCO WITH SAFFRON RISOTTO (PAGE 81)

SIDE

ROCKET, PEAR & RICOTTA FRITTER SALAD (PAGE 87)

DESSERT

CHOCOLATE HAZELNUT PUDDINGS WITH CRÈME ANGLAISE (PAGE 111)

LAZY SUNDAY BARBECUE FOR 8

Cook the salmon in a large doubled aluminium disposable roasting tray on a covered barbecue with the hood down on a medium barbecue for the same time as the oven. Once cooked, rest the salmon and beef for up to 30 minutes.

MAIN

ROAST SALMON WITH FENNEL & APPLE SALAD (PAGE 12)

BARBECUED BEEF RUMP WITH PANZANELLA (PAGE 16)

SIDE

COS HEARTS WITH GREEN GODDESS DRESSING (PAGE 86)

DESSERT

CARAMEL & PEANUT BUTTER MOUSSE MERINGUE CAKE (PAGE 118)

COS HEARTS WITH GREEN GODDESS DRESSING (PAGE 118)

FIG & DATE TARTS (PAGE 108)

GRAZING MENU FOR 16

Serve the vegetable pie and empanadas with drinks while your guests are standing then present the buffet items and dessert bar on a table for people to help themselves. You could also serve the tart with vanilla ice-cream and seasonal berries.

TO HAVE WITH DRINKS

GREEN VEGETABLE PIE WITH YELLOW SPLIT PEA DIP (PAGE 48)

SPICY BEEF EMPANADAS (PAGE 35)

BUFFET

LAMB RAGÙ MOUSSAKA (PAGE 77) (DOUBLE THE RECIPE)

GREENEST GREEN SALAD (PAGE 40)

DESSERT BAR

FIG & DATE TARTS (PAGE 108)

ROSEWATER & PISTACHIO CHEESECAKE CUPS (PAGE 130)

GLOSSARY

ALLSPICE also known as pimento or jamaican pepper; available whole or ground. Tastes like a blend of clove, cinnamon, and nutmeg – all spices.

ALMONDS
flaked paper-thin slices.
ground also called almond meal; nuts are powdered to a coarse flour-like texture.
slivered small pieces cut lengthways.

BAKING PAPER also called parchment paper or baking parchment – is a silicone-coated paper that is primarily used for lining baking pans and oven trays so cakes and biscuits won't stick, making removal easy.

BEANS
borlotti also called roman beans or pink beans, can be eaten fresh or dried. Interchangeable with pinto beans due to their similarity in appearance – pale pink or beige with dark red streaks.
haricot the haricot bean family includes navy beans and cannellini beans. All are mild-flavoured white beans which are interchangeable.

BREADCRUMBS, PANKO (JAPANESE) have a lighter texture than Western-style breadcrumbs. They are available from most supermarkets and Asian food stores.

BRIOCHE French in origin; a rich, yeast-leavened, cake-like bread made with butter and eggs. Available from cake or specialty bread shops.

BUK CHOY also called bok choy, pak choi, chinese white cabbage or chinese chard; has a fresh, mild mustard taste.

BUTTER we use salted butter unless stated otherwise; 125g is equal to 1 stick (4 ounces).

CAPERBERRIES olive-sized fruit formed after the buds of the caper bush have flowered; are usually sold pickled in a vinegar brine with stalks intact.

CAPSICUM (BELL PEPPER) available in many colours: red, green, yellow, orange and purplish-black. Be sure to discard seeds and membranes before use.

CHEESE
kefalotyri a hard, salty cheese made from sheep and/or goat's milk. Its colour varies from white to yellow depending on the mixture of milk used in the process and its age. Great for grating over pasta or salads. Can be replaced with parmesan.
mascarpone an Italian fresh cultured-cream product made in much the same way as yoghurt. Whiteish to creamy yellow in colour, with a buttery-rich, luscious texture. Soft, creamy and spreadable, it is used in Italian desserts and as an accompaniment to fresh fruit.
ricotta a soft, sweet, moist, white cow's-milk cheese with a low fat content and a slightly grainy texture.

CHICKEN
maryland leg and thigh still connected in a single piece; bones and skin intact.
thigh fillets thighs with the skin and bone removed.

CHILLI, JALAPEÑO pronounced hah-lah-pain-yo. Fairly hot, medium-sized, plump, dark green chilli; available pickled, sold canned or bottled, and fresh, from greengrocers.

CHINESE COOKING WINE (SHAO HSING) also called chinese rice wine; made from fermented rice, wheat, sugar and salt. Found in Asian food shops; if you can't find it, use mirin or sherry.

COCOA, DUTCH-PROCESSED is treated with an alkali to neutralise its acids. It has a reddish-brown colour, a mild flavour and is easy to dissolve.

COCONUT
cream obtained commercially from the first pressing of the coconut flesh alone, without the addition of water; the second pressing (less rich) is sold as coconut milk. Available in cans and cartons at most supermarkets.
desiccated unsweetened, dried and finely shredded coconut flesh.
flaked dried flaked coconut flesh.
milk not the liquid found inside the fruit (coconut water), but the diluted liquid from the second pressing of the white flesh of a mature coconut. Available in cans and cartons at most supermarkets.

CORNFLOUR (CORNSTARCH) available made from corn (maize) or wheat; used as a thickening agent in cooking.

CREAM
thick (double) a dolloping cream with a minimum fat content of 45%.
thickened (heavy) a whipping cream that contains a thickener. It has a minimum fat content of 35%.

CRÈME FRAÎCHE a mature, naturally fermented cream (minimum fat content 35%) having a velvety texture and slightly tangy, nutty flavour. Crème fraîche, a French variation of sour cream, can boil without curdling and be used in sweet and savoury dishes.

COUSCOUS a fine, dehydrated, grain-like cereal product made from semolina; it swells to three or four times its original size when liquid is added.

DAIKON also called white radish; this long, white horseradish has a wonderful, sweet flavour. After peeling, eat it raw in salads or shredded as a garnish; also great when sliced or cubed and cooked in stir-fries and casseroles. The flesh is white but the skin can be either white or black; buy those that are firm and unwrinkled from Asian food shops.

EGGPLANT also known as aubergine. Ranging in size from tiny to very large and in colour from pale green to deep purple.

FENNEL also called finocchio or anise; a crunchy green vegetable slightly resembling celery that's eaten raw in salads; fried as an accompaniment; or used as an ingredient. Also the name given to the dried seeds of the plant which have a stronger licorice flavour.

FLOUR, PLAIN (ALL-PURPOSE) unbleached wheat flour; is the best flour for baking.

GELATINE powdered gelatine; is also available in sheet form known as leaf gelatine. Three teaspoons of dried gelatine (8g or one sachet) is about the same as four gelatine leaves.

HARISSA a Moroccan paste made from dried chillies, cumin, garlic, oil and caraway seeds. Available from Middle-Eastern food shops and supermarkets.

HORSERADISH CREAM a commercially prepared creamy paste consisting of grated horseradish, vinegar, oil and sugar.

KOHLRABI member of the cabbage family; this purple or green bulb with smaller, leafy stems sprouting from the top, looks like a root vegetable and is solid like one, but is crisper in texture with a delicate cauliflower/turnip flavour.

KUMARA (ORANGE SWEET POTATO) Polynesian name of an orange-fleshed sweet potato often confused with yam.

LAMB, BACKSTRAP also called eye of loin; the larger fillet from a row of loin chops or cutlets. A tender cut, so is best cooked rapidly: barbecued or pan-fried.

LEMON GRASS a tall, clumping, lemon-smelling and tasting, sharp-edged aromatic tropical grass; the white lower part of the stem is used, finely chopped. Can be found fresh, dried, powdered and frozen, in supermarkets, greengrocers and Asian food shops.

MAPLE SYRUP distilled from the sap of sugar maple trees found only in Canada and the USA. Maple-flavoured syrup or pancake syrup is not an adequate substitute for the real thing.

MIZUNA Japanese in origin; the frizzy green salad leaves have a delicate mustard flavour.

MUSHROOMS, SWISS BROWN also known as roman or cremini. Brown mushrooms with full-bodied flavour.

ONION
green (scallions) also called, incorrectly, shallot; an immature onion picked before the bulb has formed, has a long, bright-green stalk.
shallots also called french or golden shallots or eschalots; small and brown-skinned.

POLENTA a ground, flour-like cereal made of dried corn (maize). Also the name of the dish made from it.

POMEGRANATE MOLASSES not to be confused with pomegranate syrup or grenadine (used in cocktails); is thicker, browner and more concentrated in flavour — tart, sharp, slightly sweet and fruity. Brush over grilling or roasting meat, seafood or poultry, add to salad dressings. Buy from Middle Eastern food stores or specialty food shops.

RICE, ARBORIO small, round grain rice well-suited to absorb a large amount of liquid; the high level of starch makes it especially suitable for risottos, giving the dish its classic creaminess.

SAFFRON stigma of a member of the crocus family, available ground or in strands; imparts a yellow-orange colour to food once infused. The quality can vary greatly; the best is the most expensive spice in the world.

STAR ANISE dried star-shaped pod with an astringent aniseed flavour; used to flavour stocks and marinades. Available whole and ground, it is an essential ingredient in five-spice powder.

STERILISING JARS it's important the jars be as clean as possible; make sure your hands, the preparation area, tea towels and cloths etc, are clean, too. The aim is to finish sterilising the jars and lids at the same time the preserve is ready to be bottled; the hot preserve should be bottled into hot, dry clean jars. Jars that aren't sterilised properly can cause deterioration of the preserves during storage. Always start with cleaned washed jars and lids, then follow one of these three methods:
(1) Put the jars and lids through the hottest cycle of a dishwasher without using any detergent.
(2) Lie the jars down in a boiler with the lids, cover them with cold water then cover the boiler with a lid. Bring the water to the boil over a high heat and boil the jars for 20 minutes.

(3) Stand the jars upright, without touching each other, on a wooden board on the lowest shelf in the oven. Turn the oven to the lowest possible temperature, leave the jars to heat through for 30 minutes. Remove the jars from the oven or dishwasher with a towel, or from the boiling water with tongs and rubber-gloved hands; the water will evaporate from hot wet jars quite quickly. Stand the jars upright and not touching each other on a wooden board. Fill the jars as directed in the recipe; secure the lids tightly, holding jars firmly with a towel or an oven mitt. Leave the preserves at room temperature to cool before storing.

SUGAR
brown a very soft, finely granulated sugar that retains molasses for its colour and flavour.
caster (superfine) finely granulated table sugar.
icing (confectioners') also known as powdered sugar; pulverised granulated sugar crushed together with a small amount of cornflour (cornstarch).
palm also called nam tan pip, jaggery, jawa or gula melaka; made from the sap of the sugar palm tree. Light brown to black in colour and usually sold in rock-hard cakes; use brown sugar instead.

TAMARIND CONCENTRATE (OR PASTE) the distillation of tamarind pulp into a condensed, compacted paste. Thick and purple-black, it requires no soaking. Found in Asian food stores.

VANILLA
bean paste made from vanilla beans and contains real seeds. Is highly concentrated: 1 teaspoon replaces a whole vanilla bean. Found in most supermarkets in the baking section.
extract obtained from vanilla beans infused in water; a non-alcoholic version of essence.

ZUCCHINI also called courgette; small, pale- or dark-green or yellow vegetable of the squash family. Harvested when young, its edible flowers can be filled and deep-fried.

CONVERSION CHART

MEASURES

One Australian metric measuring cup holds approximately 250ml; one Australian metric tablespoon holds 20ml; one Australian metric teaspoon holds 5ml.

The difference between one country's measuring cups and another's is within a two- or three-teaspoon variance, and will not affect your cooking results. North America, New Zealand and the United Kingdom use a 15ml tablespoon.

All cup and spoon measurements are level. The most accurate way of measuring dry ingredients is to weigh them. When measuring liquids, use a clear glass or plastic jug with the metric markings.

The imperial measurements used in these recipes are approximate only. Measurements for cake pans are approximate only. Using same-shaped cake pans of a similar size should not affect the outcome of your baking. We measure the inside top of the cake pan to determine sizes.

We use large eggs with an average weight of 60g.

DRY MEASURES

METRIC	IMPERIAL
15g	½oz
30g	1oz
60g	2oz
90g	3oz
125g	4oz (¼lb)
155g	5oz
185g	6oz
220g	7oz
250g	8oz (½lb)
280g	9oz
315g	10oz
345g	11oz
375g	12oz (¾lb)
410g	13oz
440g	14oz
470g	15oz
500g	16oz (1lb)
750g	24oz (1½lb)
1kg	32oz (2lb)

LIQUID MEASURES

METRIC	IMPERIAL
30ml	1 fluid oz
60ml	2 fluid oz
100ml	3 fluid oz
125ml	4 fluid oz
150ml	5 fluid oz
190ml	6 fluid oz
250ml	8 fluid oz
300ml	10 fluid oz
500ml	16 fluid oz
600ml	20 fluid oz
1000ml (1 litre)	1¾ pints

LENGTH MEASURES

METRIC	IMPERIAL
3mm	⅛in
6mm	¼in
1cm	½in
2cm	¾in
2.5cm	1in
5cm	2in
6cm	2½in
8cm	3in
10cm	4in
13cm	5in
15cm	6in
18cm	7in
20cm	8in
22cm	9in
25cm	10in
28cm	11in
30cm	12in (1ft)

OVEN TEMPERATURES

The oven temperatures in this book are for conventional ovens; if you have a fan-forced oven, decrease the temperature by 10-20 degrees.

	°C (CELSIUS)	°F (FAHRENHEIT)
Very slow	120	250
Slow	150	300
Moderately slow	160	325
Moderate	180	350
Moderately hot	200	400
Hot	220	425
Very hot	240	475

INDEX